PARA-URBAN
DETECTIVE

a memoir

Norman R. Gagnon

Para-Urban Detective

A memoir

ISBN 9798479625480

First Edition

Published by Kindle Direct Publishing

About this cute little guy…

There are four action words that ignite my soul: Travel, Explore, Discover, and Investigate. These inspiring verbs became my creed sort to say, as I plan my expeditions. The acronym "T E D I" was conceived during the writing of this book, and a sketch of this teddy bear soon followed. This iconic character also conjures up a brave and avid adventurer, explorer, and America's 26th commander-in-chief: *"Get action. Seize the moment. Man was never intended to become an oyster"*- President Theodore Roosevelt.

TO LEO,

Table of Contents

Preface

In August of 1973, I was in my early teens and was spending two adventurous weeks of my school summer vacation at my cousin Rémy's homestead in Québec, Canada. On a beautiful cloudless afternoon, we were energetically pedaling our bikes back from exploring a lake at the end of Rang Quatre; the "fourth row" of a series of unpaved country roads that branched out from the main thoroughfare. As we approached his farmhouse, something extremely brilliant caught my eye that was gleaming on top of one of the utility poles. When I tried to point this out to him, an explosion occurred! Almost falling off our bikes, we locked our brakes and remained frozen for a few seconds. I shouted at Rémy as I pointed upward to what I saw on top of the pole that looked like a welder's torch flare that appeared just a few seconds before the blast.

We carefully looked around for debris such as a loose cable or even some evidence of a blown transformer, but everything was intact. Confused and shaken about what had taken place, Rémy and I hopped back onto our bikes and quickly peddled to the front porch of his house. We jumped off our bikes and ran inside to see if there was power. Oui, the house had electricity.

Today, I still do not know what caused this detonation on top of this wooden electric pole on this eventful August day. Possibly it was a wake-up call for me...but to what exactly?

Now as an adult, I have likewise experienced many unusual incidents that have compelled me to delve into otherworldly happenings a little deeper. I have learned to apply the streetwise skills that I have acquired over the years to investigate similar reports of paranormal phenomena. I also take the time to support other people who have experienced things that they cannot explain. Sometimes the best way to help somebody who has come face to face with strange incidents is to simply listen to their story over a cup of coffee.

My life's journey within these extraordinary treks is like the small carbon-steel pinball being bounced around from one meaningful synchronicity to another, picking up a little mystic byproduct from the bumpers and rubber flippers. Now I believe that it is time to let the ball drop down the hole, to gather my thoughts, and to finally share what I have experienced so far.

I wrote this book to disclose some of the most intriguing cases that I have examined, covering more than two decades of investigating haunted establishments, unidentified aerial phenomena, and a few extraordinary events that just don't fit precisely into any paranormal category.

In chapter eleven's 'Travel Log', you will experience some of the most noteworthy destinations I've visited since I was a teenager, along with the interesting regional cuisine I have sampled during my travels.

You will also gain a pretty good perspective of what makes me tick...to the 'tic tac' UFOs that were recently tracked by a U.S. Navy fighter jet with advanced technologies built by the very same global aerospace and defense company that I am currently employed with. This stuff is pretty much the *Norm* in my life (yes, pun intended).

Forewords

Richard Southall: Author of *'How to be a Ghost Hunter'* and *'Haunted Route 66'*

When Norman approached me in late 2019 to review his book with the working title of *Para-urban Detective* I had no idea as to what I was signing up for. I was simply helping a friend out by editing his first book; I did so because I remember the excitement and enthusiasm of writing my book *'How to Be a Ghosthunter'* several years ago.

Soon after I read the first draft of *Para-urban Detective, a memoir*, I realized that I was reading something special. It was not only an autobiography; it was a glimpse into the life of the most authentic people I have ever known. I am glad to call Norman a friend and colleague in the world of the unknown.

Norman has spent his entire life investigating what makes up the world around him. Whether it be the synchronicities that introduced him to the paranormal, his job at local security firms, working on movie sets and being featured as an expert on paranormal television shows, his involvement with Mutual UFO Network, and his own personal endeavors, Norman has embraced his inquisitive nature and sought answers to questions that have been asked by people for hundreds of years. That question is,

"I know how something happens. Now, I want to know *why* it happens." His attempts to answer those questions have introduced him to many new friends and colleagues; it has also sent him on adventures to remote and exotic locations on three continents. To me, that is the ultimate dedication to finding the truth and answering the 'why' question.

I now invite you to sit back, relax, and read Norm's book. It will give you a glimpse into the life of a self-made adventurer, paranormal investigator, and 'para-urban detective'. I hope that *'Para-urban Detective – a Memoir'* will inspire you to do your own investigations of not only the paranormal but all parts of the world around you.

***

Barry Fitzgerald: Formerly of Ghost Hunters International (GHI) TV series, Author, Photographer

We roll into this life through birth and for the most part, try and live our best through it and finally return to the darkness. Some would say an open and shut case, however, what if life isn't as simple as that? I have met Norman along with a team of American ghost hunters back in 2006, for a week as they investigated a few of our haunted castles and explore other ancient sites.

At the time, I was their private guide and driver of a large passenger van that sat all of these ghost hunters quite comfortably as we explored my home throughout Ireland.

Within this life, the picture can become wrinkled and holes can appear in our paradigm in which some would simply try and iron out and get on with life as best they could, whilst for others, sometimes they will stop and possibly ponder the mystery in the hole before moving on with life, whilst a smaller group of people will climb into the hole.

This life is far from straightforward, and for those souls who descend into that rabbit hole, it is the responsibility of those who went before them to leave clues of what to expect. Understanding our past through our ancestral and archeological past is vital in a world in which we share with other beings. The further we go back the harder the records are to decipher, Ireland's primal history begins with ancient stone carvings etched on huge standing stones dotted across the landscape some 5,500 years ago, but the involvement of man on the island stretches further into the past to 14,000BC, around the same time the great temple of Gobekli Tepe was being built in Southern Turkey. On these ancient stones are carved the clues to a race of beings that have slipped through the veil and for the most part remained out of sight, only appearing in part, leaving tales of hauntings, UFO sightings, and strange creatures.

Our ancestors experienced these beings the same way we experience them today, however, their appearance was very different. Same phenomena, different masks, is the only way to track these beings and it's a responsibility to learn from our past experiences and to have a trail of bread crumbs left for the novice investigators to follow in order for them to connect the dots and avoid the pitfalls.

Norman's book is a reflection on the need to record and share important data and makes it available to the research community. As Marcus Tullius Cicero once said, *"The safety of the people shall be the highest law."*

Chapter One: In the Beginning

"This highway leads to the shadowy tip of reality: you're on a through route to the land of the different, the bizarre and unexplainable...you're entering the wondrous dimension of imagination."
- Rod Serling, 'The Twilight Zone'

I grew up in the small town of Saint-Côme-Linière within the eastern province of Québec, Canada, right at the launch of the 1960's space-age. The regional dialect was predominantly French Québécois and nearly all the folks who lived in the area were Roman Catholic. My father, Henri-Louis Gagnon, was a retired officer in the Royal Canadian Army. Later, he became the Chief of Police and the Search & Rescue Coordinator for both our small township and the neighboring municipality of Saint-Georges de Beauce where he was stationed.

Henri-Louis Gagnon

My dad in the late 1950s, was an avid explorer

Aside from my approach to thinking 'outside the box', I believe these are the traits of his genetic blueprint that I inherited from him as well as to travel and explore boroughs that are off the beaten paths. These attributes would serve me well later in life, especially in the investigative field.

As for my mother, Vivian N. Gagnon, there was a special connection between us. As a four-year-old boy, I occasionally experienced brief "psychic hiccups" with her. For example, on one occasion I suddenly bounced off the sofa and rushed down to the basement, I breathlessly appeared in the kitchen a few moments later and handed her a small bag of potatoes. "Wow, how did you know I needed that?" she asked. With a grin, I simply shrugged my shoulders and ran back into the living room to plop down on the rug in front of the Zenith TV to resume watching my cartoons.

There were several 'insights' I experienced over my early years that my mom seemed to understand.

As a young boy, I had a very active imagination and often transferred this creative energy onto blank sheets of paper with the help of a 48-count box of crayons. One drawing my mother kept was of an outer space scene with a handful of colorful planets, with a single rocket ship blasting away from Earth as a flying saucer zoom into the background near the planet Mars.

My creative vigor often transferred into my nighttime dreams as well. Although most of my dreams were ordinary, there were a couple of lucid nightmares that I recall even to this day. One terrifying dream involved distant trees that uprooted themselves and staggered toward my home as I helplessly watched through my bedroom window. As for a young boy's limited French, I tried to describe these creatures to my mom. I called them *"Les bibittes a poteau"* (totem pole creepy-crawlies). However, my French description did not sound too fear-provoking but rather gave her the giggles.

Another frightening reverie I recall as a child is of waking up in the middle of the night to see a strange figure standing in the shadows next to my bedroom window. As I focused my eyes on this silhouette, it sprang forward a few feet using its hind legs as it lurched close toward my bed! I looked at it long enough to realize that it wasn't human and I quickly threw the sheets over my head. About a minute later, I peeked through a small opening of my blanket and thankfully it was gone. I recall telling my mother about this the very next morning. "It looked like a large grasshopper with a head of a man grinning, with very large fish-like eyes and it had a crown or horns around its head". I do not remember her entire reaction, but I did notice that she did not giggle this time.

Today I still wonder how I, a very young boy, could ever imagine such bizarre monsters, especially in the early 1960s. As for this horned creature that has manifested itself in my bedroom, to some degree, it seems to fit the Canadian First Nations people's description of their legendary wendigo beast. Was this a glimpse of things yet to come in my life's supernatural passage?

Sadly, I was nine years old when my father passed away of thymic cancer in 1969 when he was only thirty-six years old. His untimely death changed our family's path forever. Our wonderful residence had to be sold and our loving British Shorthair grey cat was given away. My mother, older brother Danny, baby brother Marc, and I left the only home I knew in a packed 1967 Beaumont Station Wagon and drove easterly across the border to Rockville, Maryland. Months earlier, my father's younger brother Uncle René, had arranged a small house in Rockville that we could move in. Uncle René also stayed in the guest room for a few years to help us with home repairs, lawn care, and be a father-like figure.

Although I acclimated to my new surroundings rather quickly, I did hit a few rough spots along the way, especially in middle school. I was bullied by a few local boys. I remember one time as I was exploring, I was beaten up pretty badly because I walked through a neighborhood in a not-so-good area of town. These clashes with the tormenters affected my grades and overall demeanor. My mother noticed the personality changes and with the help of my Uncle René, they decided to try a different approach.

They made the decision to transfer me to a private school - Linton Hall Military Academy, for two years. This change of venue drastically improved my overall academic achievements and total outlook toward life.

In my second year at the Linton Hall, I was promoted from Sergeant to Lieutenant. In the spring of 1976, the academy held a large neighborhood yard sale in the gymnasium on campus. This one Saturday, local residents brought their odds and ends to sell. The cadets were on standby to assist with the setting up of the tables and help folks carry boxes to and from their vehicles. I remember looking around the different booths to see if anybody needed assistance and found myself at the rear of the gym. Among the stands that had been set up, one table caught my attention. This tabletop was stacked high with dozens of old books, but nobody was around.

As I walked away from this table, I heard a thump behind me. I turned around and looked down on the gymnasium floor. There I saw a vintage, dark blue book bound in cloth. I picked it up and read the title: *'Flying Saucers: Top Secret'* by Major Donald E. Keyhoe. I whispered to myself, "Wow…how cool is this", as I placed the book back on the stack.

The reverberation of this book hitting the hardwood floor seem to have rippled into my young mind to the point that I subliminally chose to do that year's upcoming science fair on the mysteries of unidentified flying objects. My tri-fold display may have been short in experiments, hypothesis tests, and data analysis, but it did attract the attention of a lot of people. Also, having the saucer section from a cannibalized USS Enterprise model dangling by fishing line in a decorated cardboard box backed with a painted star field, this was the icing on the cake. That science project was my first paranormal "investigation" and was the beginning of many synchronistic experiences that led to many explorations that have been such a major part of my life ever since.

I left the military academy and returned to the public school system for my freshman year of high school. The subsequent period in the course of my public high school years in the late 1970s, my thirst for the mysteries of extraterrestrial life was fairly quenched from viewing Hollywood movies like *Star Wars* and *Close Encounter of the Third Kind*. I did however deviate slightly from seeking the answers to the secrets of the universe with my preoccupation with this one brown-haired girl in my homeroom class who feverishly elevated my heart rate and always left me speechless. Regrettably, I missed this train. This was a bittersweet inscrutability that took me a while to shake off.

In the course of my summer vacation breaks, I worked with my Uncle René who was a Foreman in the drywall application business. As his helper, I learned what it took to build the interior of commercial buildings and high-rises from the ground up. I also learned how to transfer the architectural drawing dimensions to building surfaces. In other words, laying out the detailed wall measurements onto the concrete floors by the usage of a chalk line or an alignment self-leveling laser, so that the partitions or other structures could be built.

After graduating from Rockville High School in 1979, I seriously considered joining the U.S. Army in their Military Police force, as I was very interested in law enforcement. However, my uncle offered me to join him in the drywall trade because he said that I had a knack for this profession. After a couple of years of being his wingman, the company sent us to our latest site in Washington D.C. to an eight-story building that was in need of major renovation. After our walkthrough, he unexpectedly flung a rolled-up set of blueprints at me and said that I was ready to take charge of my own building as a Foreman! I was first startled but pleasantly surprised, and I accepted the mission!

As for my law enforcement aspirations, I still felt the need to learn more about this discipline, specifically in the detective field. I first tried a correspondence course that focused on the essentials of private investigation, which kept me busy in the evenings.

On January 13, 1982, at the same Washington D.C.

construction site, I found myself in the middle of a major snowstorm waiting on much-needed construction materials to be delivered to my building. However, the company truck that I was expecting was a no-show. I did not happen to have one of those bulky 'portable' $4000 Motorola cellphones that were just starting to be introduced in the market. So, I had to wait until I had access to a landline to find out what happened to my delivery. I later guessed that the truck was delayed because of the heavy snowfall.

It took me a couple of hours to drive through the thick snow and heavy traffic. I finally got home and turned on the TV to catch up on the local news. I saw that the Washington D.C.'s 14th Street Bridge got hit by the Air Florida Flight 90 airliner before it plunged into the icy Potomac River below. To my astonishment, one of seven occupied vehicles that got struck by the jet's fuselage was our company's 33,000-pound boom truck crane. I recall seeing news footage showing our red truck resting at a 45-degree angle against the bridge's retaining wall! My friend Grant, the driver of the company truck, was interviewed by the news reporter about the crash. He was visibly shaken but was unharmed, and I was glad he was ok.

That evening after a long phone call with my superintendent to prepare for the work week ahead, it was finally time to hit the sack. Prior to falling asleep, I suddenly remembered the dream I had from the night before. I was simply standing on the shore of a waterway looking at the debris floating on the surface of this substantial river as far as I could see. At that moment, I made the connection from the dream I had 14 hours earlier to the horrible plane disaster. I do not believe this dream was a premonition as such, but nonetheless, it was a very interesting synchronicity.

One of my hobbies at that time was creating costumes, creature suits, and scratch-built weaponry that portrayed characters from my favorite science fiction movies to be worn at Sci-Fi conventions. These were skills I developed working in theater plays during my military academy and high school years. At these conventions, I have met many folks that had the same passion as I had. Eventually, I ended up making custom science fiction props and realistic gadgets for fans and collectors that attended these sci-fi get-togethers in what is now known as 'cosplay'.

My prop fabrication and carpentry skills in that time caught the attention of local film producers as well. In 1983, I was offered the chance to work as a set builder and prop maker for a science-fiction space adventure movie called Outerworld (aka Beyond the Rising Moon) that was written and directed by Phillip J. Cook. So, I traded in my tool belt for...Orion's Belt so to speak. My first freelance cinematic gig lasted about two years. Being part of the movie industry has opened a revolving door for me and I have been on-call since. Since Outerworld, I have worked in over twelve films and TV serving in various capacity including model making, stunts, and acting.

16

Behind the scenes on the movie set of Outerworld (1984)

My thirty-plus year experience in the "movie magic" arena has also given me a keen eye for identifying and debunking fake video footage of unearthly anomalies that have inundated the YouTube platform; recordings of UFO zooming across a cityscape, or a blurry video of an alleged Sasquatch slightly concealed behind some shrubbery that a videographer claim to be legitimate. In most cases, these 'real' sightings are anything but authentic.

Back to the filming of 'Outerworld'. Approximately a year into production, I still had a strong yearning to learn more about the investigation field. The correspondence course I took earlier was a very good start, but I needed much more to quench this thirst. In the fall of 1984, I decided to work on acquiring a private investigator license through the state of Virginia. The Virginia Department of Criminal Justice Services' certified Private Investigator training course was a 60-hour program that took about ten days to complete. My classes were held at a local security investigative agency in Mclean, Virginia. In addition to this course, I received some personal tutoring in the 'tricks of the trade' from one of my classmates, a retired FBI Special Agent.

After I passed the exam with flying colors, I submitted my application and fingerprint cards to the Virginia DCJS. My Private Investigator license arrived in the mail about a week later. Within days, I accepted my first case from the same agency I took the course from. Ever since most of my cases were undercover, surveillance, and data collection. As exciting as this was, the cases were few and far between and the movie production shoot was in its final phase. I needed full-time employment soon!

In early 1985, I applied for a job at the security guard agency Wells Fargo Guard Services in Maryland, where I was hired as a Security Officer. During this time, I felt that I was gravitating towards northern Virginia, so I moved out of the state of Maryland to the other side of the Capital Beltway to Alexandria, Virginia. I was also on call in the evenings for any private investigations that were thrown my way.

A Need to Know

"When convention and science offer us no answers, might we not finally turn to the fantastic as a plausibility?" – Fox Mulder, 'The X-Files'

In February of 1985, I was granted a secret clearance by the Defense Investigative Service Clearance Office and was promoted to the day shift lead Security Officer at the headquarters of Braddock, Dunn & McDonald (BDM), a defense contractor that was located off the beltway in McLean, Virginia, and I have been with this company for 13 years.

One of my responsibilities was to ensure that anybody who walked through the lobby doors had authorized clearance or special access to be in this facility. Most visitors to BDM were engineers, consultants, and high-ranking military personnel who would often utilize our Sensitive Compartmented Information Facility (SCIF) for their classified meetings. One of these secured rooms was located on our basement level.

Braddock, Dunn & McDonald (BDM) in McLean, VA 1987

One morning I spotted BDM's president and CEO Earle C. Williams walk through the front doors of the building. He was followed by a few employees to the elevator. I noticed that he dashed by me without having his employee badge in plain sight, which was protocol for anybody entering the building. These were the times that an officer had to be courteous and more importantly do everything to avoid humiliating any top-ranking personnel. I turned around to face the employees and as Mr. Williams and I locked eyes, I raised my right hand and tapped my chest twice. He immediately recognized the meaning of my silent gesture and pulled his badge out of his shirt pocket. We exchanged smiles as the elevator doors closed. I thought to myself, "I'm keeping this job for a while."

20

Shaking hands with BDM CEO Earle C. Williams in 1992 at his retirement party.

During this time my interest in UFOs, ESP, and Bigfoot were marginal due to the fact that there were very few television programs covering these subjects. However, on occasion, I would find fascinating shows such as "In Search Of" and various old documentaries on mysterious creatures that were captured on shaky black & white 16mm film. I had collected a small assortment of books including "Uri Geller, My Story" and Erich von Däniken "Chariots of the Gods". I had also put together a compilation of late 1970s and early 1980s National Enquirer newspaper clippings on the paranormal. To round out my collection, I had bought some UFO-related magazines from my local Peoples Drug pharmacy.

As a security officer, my job was to process exclusive

intelligence officials from Fort Meade, Stanford Research Institute (SRI), the Defense Intelligence Agency (DIA), and several other related agencies. Little did I know that literally right under my feet these men were working on highly classified research developments related to everything from extrasensory perception to remote viewing for intelligence-gathering purposes. The results of this covert research led to the creation of a special team known as the UFO Working Group whose main purpose was to examine reports of unidentified flying objects and related subject matter. Reliable and current sources also disclosed to me that even the subject of livestock mutilations was one topic that these agencies were interested in.

Looking back, I can remember one unusual episode very clearly. I was sitting at the lobby's front desk having a cup of coffee to help me through my double shift. I was just about to take a sip of the coffee when I noticed that it started to vibrate rhythmically. In retrospect, the vibration reminded me of the scene from *Jurassic Park* when the boy noticed the water glass on the dashboard ripple as the tyrannosaurus rex slowly stomping towards the vehicle. This caught my attention and I thought to myself, "What the hell is this?" I later shared my strange experience with the evening security manager Bob M. as he walked by. After I described what had happened to my cup of coffee, I asked, "What's going on with this building?" Bob's face immediately turned red with disbelief.

He hastily replied, "This is none of our business!" Then he suddenly turned around and walked away. This interaction was a learning experience, if one is employed by a company that is secretly developing emerging technologies, one must not ask what is "behind the curtain".

The classified United States Army programs that were taking place in my building (and undoubtedly in other parts of the country) went by a number of different codenames until the 1990s. At this point, all of the various endeavors merged and became known as the 'Stargate Project'. I recall one of the men who attended most of our BDM meetings was United States Army Colonel John B. Alexander. He was a decisive figure in the field of non-lethal weapons and classified paranormal projects. The group that he led was called Advanced Theoretical Physics (ATP). According to Colonel Alexander's 2011 book *UFOs: Myths, Conspiracies, and Realities*, some of the classified meetings that took place in my building were on the UFO phenomenon.

I also recall times when I found myself chatting with the BDM Program Director for Intelligence Operations, retired Army Major General Albert Stubblebine, while he waited in the lobby for his attendees to show up for these classified meetings. I would describe Stubblebine as a very tall and slim man in his late fifties. He was an out-of-the-box thinker with a close resemblance to the actor Lee Marvin. In the early 1980s (prior to joining BDM) Major General Stubblebine led a special parapsychology team for the United States Army Intelligence and Security Command (INSCOM) in Fort Belvoir, Virginia.

What took place beneath me in the basement's Sensitive Compartmented Information Facility was another one in a series of coincidences in my life, which is what I would like to call 'psychoenergetics' and interrelated controversial studies. I think that during my time at BDM, and especially after my vibrating java episode, I started to relink with the rising wave of the synchronicity curl that began when I was a child that I am still surfing it to this day.

In addition to being the lead security officer, I also worked closely with BDM Corporate Security and became friends with their staff. In particular, I became close with a man named Jeff H. and his manager, Mike T., who was a former intelligence operative. One of their tasks was to conduct TSCM (Technical Surveillance Counter-Measures) for all of the buildings within our area when called upon. One day Jeff H. completed a sweep for covert listening devices in Major General Stubblebine's office in a nearby BDM building with a non-linear Super Scout detector. He later told me that he had discovered a cigar box full of bent and twisted metal utensils that was slightly hidden in Stubblebine's bookcase. Perplexed by the discovery of this finding, he placed the box back exactly where he found it and moved on to the next office. I suspected that they were likely shiny mementos from some of the Major General's psychokinesis spoon-bending parties.

In 1995 I was promoted to BDM Corporate Security, which allowed me to be upgraded to a Top Secret clearance. I started my new position as a Classified Document Control Specialist (also known as Classified and Sensitive Material Management- CSMM). Part of my job was also to assist the Physical Security and Investigation Department at BDM's new headquarters, which was the newly built building that was just a few blocks from the one in which I started working ten years prior. Our new HQ was located right across from the CIA's Stafford Building on Westbranch Drive in McLean. This clandestine building was demolished in the summer of 2019 as part of the city's revitalization plan.

In my new position, I was also responsible for controlling communication security (COMSEC) devices such as STU-IIIs which are encrypted telephone communication systems, and related Crypto Ignition Keys (CIK). Being the COMSEC custodian, I was required to take a week-long specialized technical, operational and physical security measures training.

On my final day of the COMSEC course in Washington

D.C, I was in a large auditorium full of law enforcement and related government officials. I noticed that sitting on my left were two United States Border Patrol officers. During a break, one officer leaned over and whispered to me, "Are you with the CIA?" Surprised by this statement, I whispered "No, I am not". They both nodded and one of them whispered back "We understand".

I excused myself and went to the restroom before the break ended. I was puzzled by what had taken place with these officers. Then, as I was washing my hands I looked in the mirror and realized that I was wearing my navy blue t-shirt with the Central Intelligence Agency seal patch on the chest - a gift that I accepted from an acquaintance. I quietly laughed.

BDM provided services in such fields as advanced technology, systems engineering, applied sciences, development of weapons systems, etc. In 2015, the old and vacant BDM headquarters off Jones Branch Drive across from the McLean Hilton was demolished to make room for a more contemporary center. The lobby area where I once was a Security Officer was replaced with an upscale and stylish espresso bar at the base of a mid-rise apartment complex. A bygone environment from the Cold War era had been replaced by cold brew coffee.

Mutual UFO Network

"Learn how to see. Realize that everything connects to everything else." – Leonardo da Vinci

In 1998 I left BDM and took a position with Computer Science Corporation (CSC) working at their Arlington (Crystal City) site. I was at their facility/security department for six years performing tasks that were similar to those at my previous job at BDM. In total, I succeeded at working twenty-two years in the security industry; I also wore different hats with several different corporations while working in the nation's capital. With each position I learned a wide range of diverse skills; everything from designing custom modular/portable trade show displays, installing and testing radio frequency shielded enclosures to street level urban reconnaissance and surveillance. At this point in my life, I began to apply all of these well-honed skills to a slightly divergent vocation that I wanted to do for years– paranormal investigation!

While working with these defense contractors during the day, I spent a lot of my free time becoming more involved in my paranormal interests. I joined several related groups and spent countless hours exploring haunted establishments, investigating UFO sightings, and have often traveled to my neighboring state of Pennsylvania on many occasions to search for the elusive Sasquatch.

In 2004, I became a member of the Mutual UFO Network (MUFON) with their Virginia Chapter as a Field Investigator (FI). MUFON officially began on May 31, 1969. They first started as a US-based non-profit organization composed of civilian volunteers that originated with a small team of ufologists that later linked with the UFO group Aerial Phenomena Research Organization (APRO). They currently have more than 3,500 members both nationwide and representatives in more than 43 countries. Annual membership includes monthly e-journals, special access to members-only sections of the website, UFO reports archive, and much more.

Today, to become a MUFON Certified Field Investigator one must be able to acceptably pass a personal background check and be willing to agree to and sign a MUFON non-disclosure agreement. Folks that are drawn to this subject may first reach out and contact their state director and let them know that you are interested in becoming an investigator.

Once you've signed in as a new Field Investigator, you will need to purchase a hard copy of the MUFON Field Investigator manual or subscribe to the online FI Certification Training version by visiting the MUFON Store at their website. If one is available, you may also participate in field training conducted by your local chapter.

The course includes informational material of weather

anomalies, astronomy, conventional aircraft (especially beacon/strobe configurations), satellites, photographic equipment, evidence collection, and the basics of interviewing and report writing. Once you pass your exam and have your application and background check approved, you will be designated as a field investigator trainee. Typically they will have you work with an experienced FI on several cases before allowing you to attempt a field investigation on your own.

For myself, after being a Field Investigator with MUFON for four years, I applied to join the newly formed rapid-response Strike Team for Area Research (STAR) in early 2008. On February 11, 2008, I was appointed to this special unit. The investigators asked to join the STAR Team are selected from a pool of qualified field investigators. When a credible UFO sighting or related incident has taken place, the STAR investigators would be deployed on a few hours' notice to secure critical UFO evidence nationwide. At the beginning of this unit, the Field Investigators were also reimbursed for travel and lodging. I was one of the first STAR Team Investigators (STI) to be selected for this special unit and was the first investigator to be deployed. My first assignment as an STI was the renowned 2008 Christopher Bledsoe, Sr. abduction case in North Carolina, which will be discussed in detail in Chapter Three.

An offshoot program called the Case Assistance Group

(CAG) was established shortly after the STAR Team was formed. This group provided temporary investigative services on a global scale for regions that did not have trained UFO researchers on hand.

Here's an example of an international CAG case that was assigned to me that involved four Georgian men who had camped in the valleys of the Caucasus Mountains not far from the Russian border. Although the case was submitted to MUFON in 2014, the event took place on August 3, 1986, during the height of the Cold War, twenty-three years prior. The main witness that contacted me about his sighting, his emails were well written as he was a linguist in English. This is his report:

FINAL REPORT DATE: January 19, 2014
STAR FI/CAG ID# 10061 - Norman Gagnon
INTERNATIONAL CASE#: 53356 - Tbilisi, Georgia

SYNOPSIS: GM, a Georgian, and three other young men were camping near the area of Omalo, Tusheti. During that night, they all witnessed 4 lights flying at a distance.

OBJECT DESCRIPTION: Four bright, orange lights were seen flying in an irregular diamond formation from W/SW to an easterly trajectory, then fading behind distant mountains.

WEATHER INFORMATION: (Tbilisi) 1986 climate results for Aug. 6th only: 23.8c, max 33.4c, min 18.5c, mean visibility 15.4 (Km).

LOCATION: A country in the Caucasus region of Eurasia. Located at the crossroads of Western Asia and Eastern Europe; the capital of Georgia is Tbilisi. Georgia covers a territory of 26,911 square miles and has a population of five million people. Georgia was occupied by Soviet Russia during this period.

ACCOUNT: This historical, international sighting took place in 1986 during the height of the Cold War. The incident involved a group of campers; indigenous people who attempted to enjoy an outing among the valleys of the Georgia's Caucasus Mountains, just a few kilometers from the Russian border. But their midnight repose was interrupted by bright lights streaking across the darkened sky.

On August 3, 1986, the main witness, 25-year-old GM, his comrade Alexander M., and two other students paid a truck driver ten Soviet rubles to take them to a footpath leading to a field outside the mountain village of Omalo, Tusheti, East Georgia. GM, graduated from Tbilisi State University, is now a linguist specializing in English, and two others within his group are a physicist and a historian.

They pitched their tents on a grassy incline overlooking the ancient stone towers that dotted the rugged terrain. That evening, they enjoyed a meal of canned meat, bread, and hot tea, as the auburn sun sank behind the distant mountain range.

GM on the left, © 1986

At about 1:40 a.m. while GM was preparing his bedding, his attention was diverted southwesterly as he spotted four bright lights emerging from the nearby wooded hills and rapidly rising high above the horizon. These lights began to veer leftward toward the south-southwest as they appeared to follow the path of the Earth's curvature.

When asked to describe his experience, GM said the following. "There were four of them moving on the Earth's orbit, they glowed intensely with orange color, and they flew in a diamond-shaped pattern, but they were obviously four separate star-like objects, and no sound or noise was heard during flight. The lights eventually descended vertically then disappeared behind the eastern mountains."

Eleven other vacationers at a nearby campsite also reacted to these mysterious lights as cries were heard while arms stretched out pointing at the sky. GM talked about the other eyewitnesses during the interview. "Our neighbors saw these lights too. At that time period, we still lived in the former Soviet Union, and I thought we could have witnessed the beginning of a nuclear conflict…and we were relieved to see no explosions after the lights disappeared beyond Mount Diklosmta over the border of Chechnya."

GM and his compatriots afterward writhed back into their tents, had snifters made of vodka & honey, and before long, lanterns were turned off. They all soon fell asleep.

ADDITIONAL DETAILS: GM did not report the incident to anyone since he did not see the point in doing so. He had no proof and was sure nobody would believe him. He also added that it was not unusual for the former Soviet Union state-controlled media to suppress such an event if anyone would have dared to contact the officials. Lastly, GM shared his views of the UFO phenomena. "My standpoint concerning the UFOs is that I think they are real. I became convinced of their existence back in 1986. I always try to be scientific in my attitudes, logically these lights were moving in a fixed flight formation, and consequently, they must have been devices directed by some intelligent beings."

CONCLUSION: I have determined from our in-depth email exchanges that GM along with 14 other witnesses, all observed the same "unidentified flying lights", an event that lasted approximately three minutes.

BIGELOW AEROSPACE
ADVANCED SPACE STUDIES ®

STAR Impact Project (SIP)

March of 2009, MUFON signed a contract with Bigelow Aerospace Advanced Space Studies (BAASS) subcontracting MUFON STIs for special field investigations. The funded investigators were available to conduct inquiries related to Close Encounters of the Second Kind (lights or objects that have landed or have affected the immediate physical environment) and Third Kind (observation of or interaction with beings, entities, including telepathic communication, etc.) within 24 hours of the occurrence. We were also given a per diem to cover travel-related expenses. The SIP investigator's final reports, information, and material derived from these services were shared with BAASS. March 20, 2009, I accepted the position as a SIP Investigator and was assigned three high strangeness cases (See Chapter Two). The short-lived STAR Impact Project lasted from March 2009 to January 31, 2010.

This is a segment from an October 2009 letter to the team from the MUFON SIP Project Coordinator, which was an overview of this program:

"The STAR Team Impact Project (SIP) is a MUFON program funded in part by Bigelow Aerospace Advanced Space Studies (BAASS), initiated by Robert Bigelow, *where MUFON is being subcontracted to provide information on the Unidentified Aerial Phenomena (UAP) directly to BAASS. In simple terms, this means that we have a contract with BAASS and per the terms of the agreement, we provide information about sighting reports from CMS (MUFON Case Management System), in exchange for funds that are paid directly to MUFON each month."*

Investigative Training

I believe my involvement within the security sector and as a private investigator have given me a rational orientation and the skills necessary to effectively conduct thorough and unbiased investigations for over twenty years. As for MUFON, most of my cases were received by email from the State Director, Chief Investigator, and sometimes directly from HQ's Director of Investigations. These emails comprised of the case number, the witnesses' contact information, and a short summary of their sightings. Additional information and related elements of each case as sketches, photos, and videos were also available at the Case Management System.

Some assignments did require on-site investigations with my tactical bag, camera, digital recorder, etc., and excellent observation skills. On a few occasions, I have also teamed up with top Virginia Field Investigators Ben Moss and Tony Angiola on a few cases as well (both were also cast members of the History Channel series 'Hangar 1: The UFO Files'. In 2019, I chose to leave MUFON after fifteen years of service to focus on my family and to improve my work/life balance.

The UAP Correlation

I have worked for Raytheon Intelligence & Space, one of the top Aerospace & Defense companies on the globe, since 2012. The company provides advanced systems and services for commercial, military, and government customers worldwide. I still hold a clearance and I work within their facilities operations in Arlington, Virginia.

I noticed a pattern of events that revealed itself recently, inexplicably connecting the organizations that I have worked for, and the company that I am currently with, relating to the three Navy UFO videos that the Department of Defense (DoD) officially released to the public in 2017.

Advanced Aerospace Weapons System Application Program (AAWSAP)

The December 16, 2017 edition of *The New York Times* featured a revealing article about a classified Pentagon program named Advanced Aerospace Weapons System Application Program (AAWSAP).

Further research shows that the AAWSAP program was initiated in 2007 under the Defense Intelligence Agency (DIA) and ended five years later in 2012. The AAWSAP mission was to investigate most aspects of paranormal-related reports, including a few visits to the notorious Skinwalker Ranch located in the Uinta Basin area of Utah.

Later, internet sources showed that a subgroup of AAWSAP called the Aerospace Threat Identification Program (AATIP) was created to focus solely on Unidentified Aerial Phenomena within the military. It was purportedly overseen by Luis Elizondo, a former administrator of the Office of the Under Secretary of Defense for Intelligence (OUSDI) who had a great interest in next-generation technology. Mr. Elizondo also had close interactions with the AAWAP program. Currently, Mr. Elizondo serves as the Director of Government Programs and Services for To the Stars Academy of Arts & Science (TTSA), which according to their website is a public benefit corporation.

A significant amount of the AAWSAP's money may have been earmarked for Bigelow Aerospace Advanced Space Studies (BAASS), directed by billionaire entrepreneur Robert Bigelow, who later hired subcontractors and solicited research for this eccentric program.

After reading this mind-blowing article about this classified

UFO program in a December 2017 article of *The New York Times* and in the *Politico* newspaper, I was curious about the identities of these unknown subcontractors that were cited in these articles. So, I took out a notepad and began to sketch a flowchart: "DIA - AATIP - Bigelow Aerospace". Soon after, it dawned on me that some of the subcontractors the article referenced may have been MUFON's STAR Impact Project team!

Without delay, I created a colorful chart featuring AATIP's Luis Elizondo photo side by side with the seal of the Defense Intelligence Agency. Next, I added a large arrow pointing downward to the Bigelow Aerospace logo. Then I added another arrow pointing to the MUFON logo next to our STAR Team triangular insignia. Finally, I posted my colorful slide on my Facebook page. A few days later and with mixed reactions, I had a couple of, "*Nah, I don't think so, Norm*" replies from friends who had read my post. Months later in 2019, after reading a few rousing internet articles about the AATIP classified program, it appeared that I was correct in making this conjecture!

In 2017, there were also UFO videos released to news media that were seen around the globe. These UAPs (Unidentified Aerial Phenomena) were captured by U.S. Navy F/A-18 fighter jets that spotted and recorded 'tic tac' shaped crafts and other unidentified aerial anomalies, off both of our Pacific and Atlantic U.S. coastlines.

Another synchronicity of events pertaining to these videos, the mysterious UAPs were tracked by F/A-18 fighters with [Raytheon] Advanced Targeting Forward Look Infrared (ATFLIR) sensors and AN/APG-79 Active Electronically Scanned Array (AESA) radars, according to several military defense-related news sources and our very own Raytheon Intelligence & Space's website article that was published on December 19, 2017! Furthermore, Raytheon continues to work closely with aircraft manufactures comprising of also the 5th generation, stealth F-35 Joint Strike Fighters, providing series of advanced, multi-dimensional capability upgrades and other classified enhancements, allowing these US fighter jets to detect and react to "adversaries" at lightning speed.

As for Bigelow Aerospace, this company is currently focusing on the development of expandable station modules and related life support structures for space habitation. A recent event, a statement released by a senior manager of Bigelow Aerospace on May 4, 2018, that detailed another multidisciplinary team that is being assembled by Bigelow to investigate unidentified aerial-related phenomena. This workforce includes military intelligence, technicians, PhD-level scientists, analysts, and translators. This investigative unit also researches poltergeist activity, strange unearthly creatures, ghosts, orbs of light, and so forth, and goes further than the usual "nuts and bolts" of unidentified crafts. It would appear that Bigelow still has a significant interest in fringe scientific investigative endeavors. Been there, done that.

Aug 14, 2020

This is from an official statement/announcement from the U.S. Department of Defense website:

> On Aug. 4, 2020, Deputy Secretary of Defense David L. Norquist approved the establishment of an Unidentified Aerial Phenomena (UAP) Task Force (UAPTF). The Department of the Navy, under the cognizance of the Office of the Under Secretary of Defense for Intelligence and Security, will lead the UAPTF.
>
> The Department of Defense established the UAPTF to

improve its understanding of, and gain insight into, the nature and origins of UAPs. The mission of the task force is to detect, analyze and catalog UAPs that could potentially pose a threat to U.S. national security.

As DoD has stated previously, the safety of our personnel and the security of our operations are of paramount concern. The Department of Defense and the military departments take any incursions by unauthorized aircraft into our training ranges or designated airspace very seriously and examine each report. This includes examinations of incursions that are initially reported as UAP when the observer cannot immediately identify what he or she is observing.

Bottom line: We are being engaged by advanced, intelligently controlled technology from an unknown derivation. The government and the military are finally admitting this. I have researched and investigated UFO/UAP reports for decades. Now as an employee of Raytheon Intelligence & Space, in terms of the company's cutting-edge innovations, it seems that I am still inaudibly and marginally involved in the overall pursuit of sensing, detecting, and monitoring these unidentified aerial phenomena.

Talk about being with the right company at the right time!

Chapter Two: MUFON UFO Cases

"As a scientist I must be mindful of the past; all too often it has happened that matters of great value to science were overlooked because the new phenomenon did not fit the accepted scientific outlook of the time." – Dr. J. Allen Hynek

Working as an investigator with MUFON for over a decade has given me ample opportunity to hone my skills as a field investigator. My main purpose with MUFON was to investigate the legitimacy of currently observed phenomena on a global level.

A substantial portion of my reports were indeed 'lights in the sky'. Others were of the variety of strange daylight objects that would hover for a few seconds and disappear in a blink of an eye. But there were a handful of reports that were intriguing enough and worth the effort for me to grab my field bag and jump into my off-road vehicle for the long drive. Below are some of the most noteworthy cases that I have had the preference to investigate. For obvious reasons, some of the witnesses' names have been changed for confidentiality purposes. There are a few cases in this chapter that are marked 'Historical' which means that the witnesses may have waited a prolonged period of time before submitting their report.

The following two historical cases took place in Fairfax County, Virginia in 1962. There were two separate eyewitnesses, who were boys living in homes less than three miles apart, yet they did not know each other. Although the first case took place in 1962, this witness waited 52 years before he submitted a report to MUFON.

MUFON Case: 67435 - Historical
Location: Fairfax County, Virginia
Date of Event: 1962
Date of Assignment: June 2014
Investigator: Norman Gagnon

In 1962, seven-year-old 'JW' and his family moved into a 1,488 square-foot family home in a good neighborhood in Vienna, Virginia. JW and his brothers were settling into their new home quite nicely. While his two younger brothers had a decked-out bunkbed, JW had a twin-size bed with the headboard pressed against the back wall next to the window.

A few weeks after the family moved into the house, JW was awakened late one night by an intense light that shone through the window and illuminated the entire bedroom. In a daze, JW's eyes adjusted to the brightness. He got out of his bed and looked over at his brothers but both were sound asleep. He then peeked out the window into his backyard and was amazed to see three small humanoids standing close to each other. Two of the beings were taller than the center one. JW reported that the trio was looking around until all three of them immediately began to gaze at him!

WITNESS DRAWING 2014

Here is an excerpt from JW's personal account of the event. "There were two tall ones, I'm guessing maybe four feet tall, and a smaller one. The smaller one was in the middle and I'm pretty sure the two tall ones were holding hands with the smaller one. I know they were looking at me. I don't recall seeing their noses, necks, or any hair or even mouths. It was like their heads just blended into the body. They were grayish-white. No clothes or anything to reveal if they were male or female as it is described nowadays. As weird as it may sound, I felt like something was telling me it was okay and not to be scared...again recalling how I felt very safe and like they were friends."

While JW was transfixed by looking at these beings, he tried to find the source of the bright light. A moment later, he spotted what appeared to be a brilliant saucer-shaped object hovering over his backyard a few feet above the ground.

Again, this is from JW's personal account from the event. "From what I could tell, the craft was about five feet off the ground and it had a dome on top, but I don't recall seeing doors or windows. On a side note, weeks later I came to realize there was an indentation in the ground exactly where the craft was but it wasn't round like appeared to be as oval. The lawn depression was there for the whole 28-plus years I lived there."

JW added that it was puzzling to him that he had no memory of how he returned to bed after he saw the beings. I asked JW if he noticed any unusual marks, cuts, or punctures on his body after the incident, but he said that there were none that he recalled.

JW chose not to reveal his sighting to anyone until decades later. He saw a UFO program on television one night and thought it would be a good time to share his bizarre childhood encounter with other people.

Historical Case #2 (Non MUFON Related)
Location: Fairfax County, Virginia
Date of Event: Summer of 1962
Direct Contact-Personal Investigation: October 29, 2016

There was a second sighting that took place just a few miles from JW's encounter during the same year. Unlike JW, who kept his encounter secret for years, the second witness contacted me directly. I first met Kent, who had become a long-time UFO researcher as a result of his 1962 experience, at a 2016 UFO Conference in North Carolina. During our meeting, Kent compared his own sighing with my Case 67435 that he read in a MUFON Journal - a MUFON members' monthly publication. This incident took place in the neighboring city of Falls Church, Virginia.

When Kent was nine years old, he lived with his family in a 1,248 square foot house right around the corner from Roswell Drive. I couldn't help but notice the irony with the street name. Kent also did not remember the exact month of the incident but he did know that it took place during a warm spring or summer night.

He shared an upstairs bedroom with his brother. As with JW, Kent recalled waking up in the middle of the night by an intense light that lit up his entire bedroom. Below is Kent's account of his own experience from 1962.

During our discussion, I asked Kent to tell me what he saw in 1963. This is what he told me. "There was a very bright light that filled the room as if a searchlight was shining through the window. I got up to look and had to shield my eyes and squint to see the lights outside. I tried to wake my brother up and even shook him, but he laid motionless. I was very upset at my brother for not waking up and was surprised my parents didn't get up as I was yelling trying to wake him."

Kent ran downstairs to the living room and walked onto the brightly lit patio facing the backyard to have a better look at what was going on. Kent said that from the patio, he observed two large bright white lights that were between 50 and 75 feet above his neighbor's yard. Based on their location in relation to the trees, Kent estimated that each oval-shaped light was probably 30 to 40 feet wide. He watched them for about thirty seconds as they remained motionless. The next thing he remembered from this incident was that he found himself back in his bed.

Kent continued telling me about the lights he saw. "It was not a dream as I know. I opened the patio door to view them. I left the door cracked open to my father's displeasure the next morning. I remember being scolded. I just can't remember getting back in bed."

Kent shared another UFO sighting that took place five years later in the summer of 1967. He was sleeping on the screen-enclosed porch that was connected to the back of the house. Around 3:00 a.m., Kent was suddenly awakened by a bright cone-shaped beam of light projected from above in his backyard.

"I woke up seeing a cone-shaped light coming down and stopping about five feet off the ground. I walked out from the porch and looked up to see a bright orange disc-shaped object above me about 75 feet in the air. The light projection was coming directly from the center of the object and the beam started to recede back up. Then the UFO started to glide away. I ran out of the house and down the street chasing it but the object disappeared as if it flew southwesterly over Shreve Road."

Kent described the orange object as having no apparent doors or openings. He noted that in both cases, the UFO was absolutely silent. However, he did notice the neighbor's dog bark during the second sighting of the orange disc.

Location: Naval Weapons Station (NWS), Yorktown, Virginia

Date of Event: February 1974

Date of Assignment: December 2015

On a cold day in February 1974 at approximately 11:30 p.m., an 18-year-old Marine Private First Class (PFC) named 'John' was returning from a one-day pass from a neighborhood pub. Once inside the complex about a quarter mile past the S3 Entrance Guard Post, John walked on a road that cuts through a wooded area toward his barracks. He was suddenly illuminated by a bright green light coming from above. He looked upward and saw a large round object hovering above the several tall fir trees that surrounded him.

John described what he saw. "I stopped walking, looked at my arms that were lit up. I turned my palms up, amazed by the glow. I looked up and saw a very large object, maybe 40 or 50 feet. What I thought was the bottom of a craft."

John described the underside of the object as completely covered with what appeared to be hundreds of small glowing fluorescent green lights that he said reminded him of bubble-wrap packing material. The next thing John remembered was that he found himself walking back toward his barracks. When he got his bearings John noticed the morning's first light; he estimated that there had been more than five hours unaccounted for!

In 2015 I was assigned to investigate John's case and was given his contact information. In December I called John, who now lived in Michigan. There was no answer, so I decided to leave a voicemail asking him to return my call. Halfway through my voicemail, John picked up the phone. His hesitation could be heard as he recounted the event that took place 41 years ago in Yorktown. John stated that he could not talk about the events at the base that night with anybody and actually had second thoughts about continuing our conversation. He then stated that he should not have submitted a report to MUFON, but I assured him that I would protect his identity by using only his first name in my final report. This reassured him and he cautiously continued our interview.

John stated that since the encounter in 1974 he has experienced waves of depression and severe headaches, which prompted him to go to the hospital to speak with a doctor. The doctor ordered a complete MRI test on John's brain.

The doctor discovered two spots located in the middle of both the left and right hemispheres of his brain. However, no further medical procedures were conducted to further diagnose the possible cause for the spots that appeared on the scan. The possibility of hypnosis was brought up to John, but he decided against going this route. I noticed that toward the end of our telephone interview, John's answers became brief, and eventually he all but stopped talking about the incident altogether. Sensing that he was getting apprehensive about continuing the interview, I delicately ended our telephone interview and thanked him for sharing his incredible experience with me.

John does not remember anything about his missing time episode from 1974 and he would prefer not to. The description of the craft projecting a beam from multi-light apparatus is comparable to another case that I investigated in Dublin, Virginia in 2015, see next case below.

MUFON Case: 70201 – Historical

Location: Dublin, Virginia

Date of Event: September 27, 1994

Date of Assignment: September 6, 2015

One of my most fascinating cases was also featured in the November 2015 issue of *MUFON Journal*. In all my years of investigating the paranormal, this particular case is perhaps the most interesting because the report was of a classic saucer-shaped UFO seen hovering above homes scanning a "beam" as if it was searching for a potential abductee.

Shortly after 9:00 p.m. on September 27, 1994, 'Jeff' left work early and proceeded to head home. After a few miles, something in the night sky caught his eye. He described it as a large star moving across the horizon. Rather than going home, Jeff decided to follow the mysterious object to get a better look. Following close behind the object, Jeff noticed that it was slowly drifting down over the edge of town. As he approached Pulaski County High School, Jeff turned into the Mountain View Drive subdivision and continued to follow the light. Jeff noticed that the object changed its course and he pulled his Chevy Cavalier to the side of the road. Jeff now saw that it was disc-shaped and was completely motionless and silent as it hovered right above a house in the distance. Suddenly, the disc emitted a bluish-white beam over the roof of the house!

When asked to describe the object during our interview, Jeff said that he was approximately fifteen yards away when he first noticed the craft, which he described as a disc-shaped object about fifty feet in diameter. He said that the entire base was filled with several bright white lights with only one red light in its center. The beam projected through what appeared to be a rectangular 'window' located at the upper part of the craft.

Jeff said that he was curious and slowly drove his car closer toward the scene of the UFO. As he did so, the craft glided away from him as if it sensed that it was being watched. Then, Jeff saw the craft glide further away toward another house and began to scan it. Jeff glanced around to see if there were any other witnesses, but he could not see anybody. He did notice that there was a car parked at the high school's parking lot. Jeff felt that the car did not belong there because the parking lot was almost always empty this late in the evening.

Illustration by Norman Gagnon 2015

Jeff described his experience. "When the car drove away, I was down in the subdivision near the houses and the UFO. I can't say if the car's headlights were on or not when it left because I was looking at it from its side but it definitely caught my attention that it was leaving."

As the car drove away from the school, the disc floated away from the subdivision toward the school before Jeff lost sight of it. He estimated that the entire encounter took place over no more than a five-minute span. The streetlights and electricity from the homes and businesses were not affected by this object.

When Jeff was asked about his thoughts regarding the event, he said, "I just wanted to add that I didn't know much about UFOs at the time this happened. The biggest thing that always bothered me about the sighting was the bluish-white beam of light it was shining on the roof. It wasn't until years later that I found out that what I saw coincides with what a lot of people that claim to have been abducted have reported. It's been over twenty years since I witnessed that event but it's something that will be etched in my memory forever."

Jeff was nineteen years old at the time of this sighting. He called the local news station and inquired if anybody had reported seeing anything strange in the area that night. Since there were no reports of any unidentified objects, Jeff decided not to pursue the event any further. Today, Jeff has an associate's degree in Police Science and has interest in pursuing a career in law enforcement.

MUFON Case: 79304 - Historical

Location: Amissville, Virginia,

Date of Event: October 8, 2014

Date of Assignment: September 21, 2016

SYNOPSIS: On October 8, 2014, at approximately 7:20 pm, witness K.M. was driving west on Lee Highway (US 211) in Rappahannock County toward Sperryville, Virginia. Less than a minute prior to driving through the intersection of Colvin Road in Amissville, K.M. witnessed three bright lights hovering above the road ahead of him.

OBJECT DESCRIPTION: K.M. described two bright yellowish-white lights accompanied by a third smaller green light, all of which appeared to be hovering over the crossroads. The UFOs slowly drifted upward and to the left of the road near the tree line.

WITNESS STATEMENTS: K.M. was asked to describe what he saw. "The lights were very bright, I could not get close enough to them but I would say they were at least 50-100' wide."

As he slowly drove forward, K.M. took several photos with his iPhone. The objects soon disappeared. After reaching his destination that evening, he had forgotten about his encounter and simply moved on with his normal life.

Two years later, K.M. replaced his old iPhone with a newer version. During the data transfer, his collection of photographs was moved to the new phone. At this point, M.K. spotted the photographs he had taken of his UFO encounter in 2014. At this point, he decided to file a report with MUFON. Looking at one photograph, K.M., remembered that there was another vehicle in front of him at the time of the sighting as they were applying their brakes, perhaps this witness hesitated to drive below these mysterious lights.

As he pulled up to the clearing near the intersection, the three lights merged into one and quickly dimmed into a small point of light then disappeared! The sighting lasted about 3 minutes and these UFOs did not interfere with the truck's electrical system. This case commanded interest from MUFON headquarters.

EVIDENCE/INVESTIGATION:

Witness photo assessment:

A side-by-side comparison of one of the witness's digital photographs (Photo A) with Google Map daylight street view of the same location was conducted to confirm that there were no street lamps, light posts, or road signs located on this stretch of Highway 211 that would reflect headlights of incoming vehicles.

An observation was made also with another shot (Photo B)

that was taken from inside his truck of the bright anomalies; these lights were captured reflecting off his vehicle's hood. This photograph also depicted the same vehicle that was in front of him cautiously pulled over to the right lane to avoid these lights.

EXIF image data recorded the display date & time of the photographs along with GPS coordinates matched what was reported to MUFON. There was a full moon on that evening located at the eastern horizon, which was in the opposite direction from the course in which he was driving.

CONCLUSIONS: K.M. was a 58-year-old architectural designer. He was completely cooperative and his position was such that his testimony along with multiple iPhone photos he submitted with his report is considered serious and credible. I do not believe these bright lights were helicopters hovering silently over Highway 211, as they mysteriously merged into one bright anomaly then disappearing.

Photo A taken by witness. Note the vehicle that is ahead applying their brakes.
MUFON CMS 2014

Photo B: Note the hood reflection of aerial anomalies at the bottom.
MUFON CMS 2014

MUFON Case: 52087 - Historical

Location: Big Stone Gap, Virginia

Date of Event: April 14, 1991

Date of Assignment: September 2014

About 9:00 p.m. on April 14, 1991, a mother and daughter in her mid-20s were driving on Route 23 from Big Stone Gap to Norton, Virginia when they saw through their windshield a large bright white light quickly drop from the sky. After it stopped, the single light split into three separate bright lights. The three lights hovered over the tree line for approximately one minute before the center light ascended into the sky. The other two lights quickly flew and merged with the center light and again became one object.

The report to MUFON was made by the daughter and witness. I was able to make contact with 'Diane' and began my typical interview protocol with questions about weather, time of day, and so forth. I then asked Diane if she or her mother witnessed any humanoids during this sighting, but they both said that they had not seen anything to that effect. I also asked if either had discovered any strange markings on their bodies such as scars, cuts, or rashes after the sighting. Diane replied, "We never thought to check."

Another question that I commonly ask during an interview

is whether the witness had a related experience in the past. Diane said that her mother and other family members had seen this type of light activity near their home in the Big Stone Gap for decades. Diane added that her cousin "Sam" (now deceased) had seen a series of strange humanoids on a few occasions as a young boy while staying at his family's cabin in Big Stone Gap. He described these humanoids as 'little blue men'. I collected as much information as possible from Diane and started a separate investigation in September 2014.

In December 2014, I submitted a supplemental report regarding Sam's 'little blue men' that he experienced in the late 1970s. Based on Diane's information, Sam experienced a number of sightings over the course of a few years. As Sam had died before I conducted the initial investigation with Diane, I was not able to personally interview him. Fortunately, Sam did share his encounters with not only Diane but with several other family members. Diane was kind enough to compile additional details from another cousin "Garry", who remembered several details that Sam had told him during that time.

Garry told Diane that the cabin where Sam had some of his experiences was located near Big Cherry Reservoir, a 2200-acre wooded area near the 250-acre Lake Keokee. Diane told me that she was about eight years old when she first heard Sam mention the 'little blue men'.

He described them as intruders who randomly showed up on the cabin's property several times.

The following excerpt was taken directly from my interview with Diane. "I do remember him saying that he had been seeing them for a few years at that time, they just keep coming back to visit him for some reason; 'I think they like my cabin', Sam once said. When he first saw them, he didn't go back to the cabin for a long time but he said he got thinking, 'Well, if they wanted to hurt me, they would have the first time I saw them.' Sam never changed his story, he swore to it until the day he died."

During the interview, Diane also remembered that Sam could not figure out how the blue humanoids' small necks could support such huge heads. She also remembered that Sam once called the creatures 'little blue devils'. Diane then told me that the family no longer owned the property where the cabin was located. She added that her family kept Sam's incidents quiet for fear that local residents would think that he was crazy.

Based on my research, I was able to determine that the entities were three to four feet tall with bluish skin and wore no clothing. Physiologically, they appeared to have large malformed heads with long thin chins, large black eyes, and small slits for the mouth and nostrils. They had long fingers, but it was uncertain as to how many fingers were on each hand. Sam also told Diane and Garry that some of the blue men had 'pot bellies'.

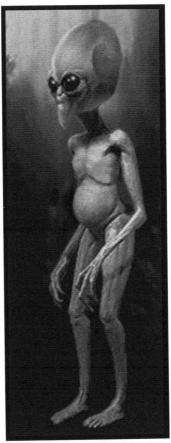

Rendition by Norman Gagnon © 2014

Interestingly enough, there have been other accounts of strange humanoids with similar features that Sam witnessed and described to his family. Specifically, the irregular proportion between the body and the cranium was quite similar to what was witnessed two years prior in Dover, Massachusetts.

In this case, according to *The Boston Globe* and other newspapers in the area on April 21 and 22, 1977 three teenage boys witnessed a strange humanoid that closely resembled those described by Sam. The three boys later submitted sketches of the creature they had seen to local authorities. Although this was an isolated event, word spread, and the creature has become known as the 'Dover Demon' within the ufology community and was featured in a number of magazines, books, and television series. As this occurred in the 1970s before the advent of the Internet, there is virtually no chance that Sam and these teenagers had either been in contact with each other or had heard of each other's accounts, especially since Sam was hesitant to tell anybody about his otherworldly visitors but to his close family members.

MUFON Case: 57661

Location: Danville, Virginia

Date of Event: July 4, 2014

Date of Assignment: July 5, 2014

Investigator: Norman Gagnon

Danville, Virginia is a small city of about 43,000 people near the North Carolina border. It is your typical all-American town and just happens to be the location of one of my most intriguing high-strangeness cases.

I received this case from a woman whom I will call Lily. She is a linguist and her husband is a therapist. She stated that the main reason she submitted a report to MUFON was because of a mysterious funnel that accompanied the UFO sighting, which was an anomaly that she had never seen before. When I first contacted Lily, I felt that she was sincere with her account and that her testimony was credible.

On July 4, 2014, at approximately 10:15 p.m., after enjoying the Independence Day fireworks at their neighborhood pavilion, Lily and her husband drove back to their home a few miles away. Before long, they pulled off of West Main Street and parked in front of their home. Once inside, Lily passed her living room window and something outside caught her attention. She looked in the night sky and observed what appeared to be a classic flying saucer with blinking and rotating lights at its base, whooshed over her house!

Bewildered, Lily looked outside and was surprised to see a dark, ominous-looking cloud swirling above. She described it as looking like a hurricane from a satellite point of view. There were also random bursts of multi-hued lights pulsing within its core. Suddenly, Lily saw two more saucers speed out of this vortex; they followed the first saucer's flight path over her house and out of sight!

65

Rendition by Norman Gagnon © 2014

This is Lily's personal account of the event. "First, I saw one flying saucer with rotating multicolor lights underneath, then two more flying saucers with the same multicolor lights underneath flew out of it. They disappeared one by one over my rooftop flying southwest. It only lasted a few seconds, maybe fifteen. Then, the hole closed and the sky looked normal again."

The appearance of these UFOs did not affect the home's electricity or electronic equipment and Lily's three cats did not react strangely during the event. Her husband was in another part of the house and did not witness the sightings.

Lily continued. "My husband was very excited but this was

not the first time he has heard about UFO sightings. I think he's more scared than anything else. He had an 'experience' when he was a teenager with a close friend of his. They witnessed some object in the sky and a huge beam of light as they were out late one night at a public park in Brooklyn, New York. They told their science teacher at their Catholic school but were deterred from going any further."

Surprisingly, during one of our email exchanges, Lily revealed to me that she had seen saucer-shaped ships like those she described in the interview when she was a child. Lily explained that she grew up in Lima, Perú with four siblings in the mid-1950s. Lily recalled that when she was six years old, she woke up in the middle of the night by an intensely bright light that pierced through her bedroom window. Lily said that the temperature became unbearably cold and at this time she noticed that some translucent beings came into view. She remembered that she felt a strong pressure all around her head. Lily explained that it felt as if she was wearing a very tight metallic band that she described as being similar to a 'crown'.

Lily shared the following details in one of her emails to me. "I remember seeing shapes of white beings, not tall but not children size, translucent almost, but not threatening at all. On the contrary, it felt soothing.

I cannot honestly say I was abducted or taken into a spaceship, I do not recall that."

When Lily shared her strange encounter with her brother and sisters at that time, she discovered that they also had early childhood memories of shadowy, white beings that visited their bedroom at night. Her younger sister, who still lives in Lima, told Lily that she vividly remembers being examined by four white, almost transparent entities.

On January 21, 2015, Lily sent me a follow-up email several months after I initially interviewed her. Here is an excerpt from that email:

"As I had mentioned before, my husband did not witness the vortex sighting but about a week later, we both saw a very high-flying UFO with multicolor lights doing 'pirouettes'. It lasted long enough for him to doubt what he was seeing, but he is reluctant to admit that it was a UFO but knows a plane could not do that kind of flying. I spoke with a couple of neighbor friends at that time. One of them saw multicolor random lights in the sky but did not pay much attention to them. I did not press any further. We relocated back to New York in October of last year (2014). Sorry, I cannot be of more help but I am completely certain of what I saw, three flying saucers coming out of a tunnel/funnel-like opening in the sky."

The following two cases included multiple unidentified 'flying triangles' that were seen by many witnesses over the sky of Virginia on the same day in September 2013. The second correlating case took place 15 hours later less than 100 miles away. The first sighting involved a "tic-tac" anomaly accompanied by six mysterious triangular UAPs that appeared to be "seeding" the sky above Roanoke. Two fighter jets were also seen flying to this location to intercept. This aerial display was observed by five witnesses.

You may think that airborne confrontation like this sounds familiar and you are correct! On November 14th, 2004, Sunday afternoon at about 2:00 p.m., two F/A-18F Super Hornet fighter jets from the USS Nimitz were on routine naval training exercise about 100 miles southwest of San Diego, California. They came face-to-face with these infamous 'tic tac' UFOs and this incident was not only detected and recorded but also the footage was released for the world to see. My case below also involves such a 'tic tac' anomaly.

MUFON Case: 51233 – First Sighting

Location: Roanoke, Virginia

Date of Event: September 24, 2013

Date of Assignment: October 1, 2013

SYNOPSIS:

"Paul", is a 49-year-old general manager at a convenience store in Roanoke. He reported that on September 24, 2013, at approximately 6:30 a.m. he observed a total of six dark gray triangles with a bright light at their center. The six objects rapidly maneuvered overhead and left behind unknown shiny dust particles.

OBJECT DESCRIPTION:

During a cigarette break, Paul saw an unusually bright light in the sky. Initially, he thought it was a star, but he soon realized that it was moving. Looking closer, Paul realized that the light was part of a triangle-shaped object's base. The triangle swiftly maneuvered in a geometrical pattern; forward, with a 90-degree turn then back again, completing the delineation. Within this outline, the UAP seemed to be expelling some sort of dull, translucent particles as it was trying to fill this area in. There was also one capsule shape (tic-tac) UFO that simply hovered near these triangles.

Paul caught the attention of a maintenance man "Gary" and

they both watched this singularity. "We watched for a few more minutes and as our eyes adjusted to the night sky, we noticed five more triangles doing the same thing at about equal distances from each other. About thirty minutes, I had brought my cashier from in the store to observe with us, along with two other customers."

At about 7:30 a.m. (around sunrise), Paul and Gary heard two jet fighters fly in very fast from the northeast, leaving contrails behind. As the fighters approached the triangle-shaped UAPs, they immediately flew off to the southwest. Paul, Gary, and the cashier also noticed another strange object at this time. Paul described it as a silver capsule that was directly overhead but at a lower altitude than the triangles. Paul: "It appeared to move slowly like a blimp at first, then rose quickly and darted off to the southwest also when the two jets got closer."

Paul added that the very next day prior to the sunrise the same three witnesses saw the triangles again for a much shorter time. After about fifteen minutes, the UAPs sped off to the north toward the Blue Ridge Mountains!

MUFON Case: 51052 (2nd Triangle Sighting)
Location: Richmond, Virginia
Date of Event: September 24, 2013
Time of Assignment: September 24, 2013

SYNOPSIS:

On September 24, 2013, an 11-year-old boy told his father that he saw UFOs. They went out in the backyard and for approximately thirty minutes, the boy and his father witnessed a fleet of about fifty triangular objects.

REPORT:

At around 8:30 p.m. an 11-year-old boy was walking his family dog in his backyard and noticed strange triangular objects flying overhead. He ran in the house and told his father about what he had just seen. Mike, a 53-year-old man, walked out to see for himself. Mike and his son both stood and watched multiple triangular objects hover above. After a short time, these unknown objects scattered apart and flew in different directions.

Mike described it like this, "It was compelling on how many they were and we could see about 6 to 8 of these triangles visible at any given time...they flew about the same height and speed to our commercial planes but there were no contrails or noise that was heard during this time."

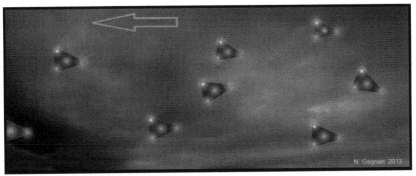

Illustration by Norman Gagnon © 2013

OBJECT DESCRIPTION:

Mike stated that the triangles were black and had red blinking lights at their centers and with lights at each corner that were blue, red, and white. These objects moved in the direction of the flat edge of the triangle; the flat side being the front of the flight trajectory and the corner point of the triangles were at the rear. The rearmost lights blinked while the front two remained steady. From the witnesses' viewpoint, these triangular objects flew very straight and steady from the southeast until they drifted out of sight toward the northeast. A group of these UFOs took about four minutes to hover across the sky until there were followed by another eight or ten of these triangular objects.

The family dog did not react strangely to these UFOs during his walk. When asked, Mike added that there were no helicopters or military jets in the area during or after this incident.

Bigelow Aerospace Advanced Space Studies - Investigations

The MUFON SIP investigators (under BAASS) were quickly dispatched to investigate reports based upon one of the three following categories:

Close Encounter of the First Kind: The witness sees a strange or unidentified light(s) or object(s) in the sky.

Close Encounter of the Second Kind: The close proximity object(s) is seen or observed to have landed on the ground or in some way has been affected the immediate physical environment.

Close Encounter of the Third Kind: The witness also experiences one or more of the following during or after the event:

A) observations of beings or entities
B) interaction with nonhuman entities
C) episodes of missing time
D) wounds or trauma to the body of unknown origin
E) taken on board a craft
F) telepathic communication
G) out-of-body experience
H) encounter with an unknown animal

The following three cases are from my Bigelow Aerospace Advanced Space Studies - STAR Impact Project (SIP) reports.

Case One

BAASS/SIP Case: 16539

Case Type: Category 2

Investigator: Norman Gagnon, MUFON S.T.A.R. FI / BAASS

Location: Residence Pasadena, Maryland

Date of Event: Thursday, April 16, 2009

Time of Event: Approximately 3:15 a.m.

BACKGROUND:

Thomas is a laboratory director and has been living in a single-family home since September 2008 with his fiancée Danielle. Both have degrees in chemistry.

UFO rendition based on the Thomas's description – 2009

Sequence of events, on-site interview:

Temperature: 39.0 degrees Fahrenheit average, visibility nine miles, wind speed 3.5 mph out of WNW and conditions: Mostly Cloudy68

On Thursday, April 16, 2009, at approximately 3:15 a.m., Danielle was awakened by a loud humming that she could not identify. She woke Thomas up to have him find out where the strange sound was coming from. Thomas walked from bedroom to bedroom to look through each window to see what was causing these strange vibrations. He thought to himself that it may be a street cleaner sweeping or possibly a utility truck working in the area. Thomas returned to the master bedroom and looked through the window that was next to Danielle when he noticed a large triangular craft hovering above. The craft was totally black with no external lights or strobes and from his point of view, it had a boomerang shape that resembled a "stretched-out" F117 Nighthawk with about a 300-foot wingspan. The hovering UFO slowly heading southeast and took about 17 minutes to pass over their house and disappear into the distance. Thomas described the humming as very loud and constant and reminded him of the sound of an electrical transformer. That Saturday, Thomas mentioned the strange incident from early Thursday morning to his neighbor Dean. Dean admitted to Thomas that he also heard the humming but was reluctant to continue the conversation.

When doing an investigation, I often will try to corroborate a person's account with additional information. This often means contacting local authorities or other people in the area who may have also encountered something out of the ordinary.

After I completed my in-person interview with Thomas, I walked toward my vehicle and noticed a parked Anne Arundel County Police Department squad car on his street. I believed that the car belonged to an officer that lived in the house where it was parked. I knocked on the officer's door but there was no answer. After I returned home, I sent two emails to the Anne Arundel County Police Department's Northern District. There was no reply to my email from the department.

I also decided to email the Anne Arundel County Department of Public Works on April 18, 2009, to enquire about whether street sweeping was done on the night of the hovering UAP incident. I received a reply on April 20, 2009, from the Department of Public Works, which simply read, *"We definitely would not sweep/clean during those hours."*

On April 21, 2009, I called the local 7-Eleven on Mountain Road, which was not too far from where Thomas lives. The store attendant, Karen, stated that nothing strange occurred on the night in question. I also called an Exxon gas station on the corner of Mountain Road and Catherine Road.

Again, the attendant said that nothing strange was heard or seen.

I emailed three local newspapers (*The Capitol Gazette*, *The Baltimore Sun*, and *The Chesapeake Bay*) about whether any UFOs had been reported but no replies were received.

Location of military bases and airports near Pasadena, Maryland: The Baltimore-Washington International Airport (BWI) is eight miles away. Fort Meade/Tipton Airport is nine miles away. Patuxent Naval Air Systems Command is approximately fifty miles south and Dover Air Force Base 95 miles to the east.

CONCLUSION:

Thomas was perplexed and a bit shook by this incident and wondered if this was a United States military aircraft and why would they build that thing and fly it in a residential neighborhood? He also stated that most of the neighbors who live on his street are either associated with the military, law enforcement agencies, or work as government contractors. I found Thomas to be very credible, had little interest in science fiction, and had little interest in anything associated with UFO phenomena.

Interestingly enough, there was another independent report that described a black, triangular craft that was seen four years prior in

Owings Mills, Maryland, which is located about twenty miles northwest from Pasadena, Maryland. This sighting took place on February 9, 2005, when witness Frank, a Lockheed Martin software engineer, saw a large triangular object flying between 500 and 800 feet above the ground.

Case Two

BAASS/SIP CASE: 18855

Case Type: Category 2

Investigator: Norman Gagnon, MUFON S.T.A.R. FI / BAASS

Location: Residence Manassas, Virginia

Date of Event: August 23, 2009

Time of Event: Approximately 3:30 p.m. EST

BACKGROUND:

On Sunday, August 23, 2009, at approximately 3:30 p.m. Rick (the first witness) was in his backyard doing yard work and his partner, Jeff (second witness) was on the roof cleaning the gutters when they both saw the same aerial incident. At the time of the event, Rick was employed as a registered nurse at a Dialysis Corporation of America office in Hyattsville, Maryland, and Jeff worked for the United States Secret Service agency.

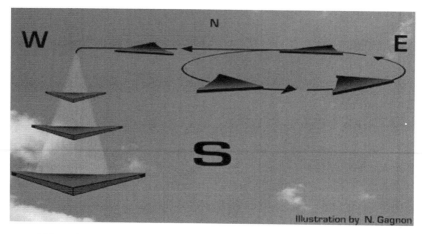

Triangular UFOs rendition based on the witnesses' description. © 2009

All of the triangles were silent and did not affect any nearby electronic or electrical equipment. No vapor trails were seen. There were no dogs in the vicinity that would have warned both of the presence of the unidentified objects. According to Rick, the objects flew below cloud level and were actually in the middle of the landing flight path for all planes approaching Dulles Airport. The entire sighting lasted about seven minutes.

CONCLUSION:

From the phone interview and the multiple emails exchanged between Jeff and me, I believe they both witnessed this aerial phenomenon, and both were very excited about what they have seen. Rick and Jeff appear to be very forthright and seem to be very stable in their professional and personal lives. Due to the nature of Jeff's career, he was trained to be acutely aware of his surroundings, as was reflected in the details he shared.

Addendum: I do not believe that these UAPs were "drones" during the time of the 2009 sighting. As Rick stated, '*they flew without sound*'. Recreational drones were available for civilian applications but much later in 2010 and became popular nationwide by 2015. Military drones would not have been flown over civilian airspace and especially in the flight path of a major international airport.

Case Three
BAASS/SIP Case: 20768
Case Type: Category 2
Investigator: Norman Gagnon, MUFON S.T.A.R. FI / BAASS
Location: Richmond, Virginia
Date of Event: November 27, 2009
Time of Event: 7:30 p.m. EST

BACKGROUND:

A neon green, teardrop-shaped UFO with a tail that emitted white flashing strobe. It was seen descending behind trees by a husband and his wife along with several other witnesses.

UFO rendition based on the Joe's description – 2009 ©

Sequence of Events:

Joe and his wife were on their way home when they stopped at a traffic light. They were about to make a left turn onto Hull Street Road (Route 360) when Joe's wife (no name given) was startled by a strange green glowing object. She pointed it out to Joe who watched the UFO descend behind some trees that were later determined to be about 320 feet away from their vehicle. At the intersection were a Hardee's restaurant and a blue-roofed motel. Joe drove into the motel parking lot near the woods where they saw the object descend. Behind the hotel was a large grassy field. From their vantage point, Joe and his wife saw the UFO descend from right to left at an approximate 45-degree angle. They watched it for four or five seconds before they lost sight of it behind some more trees. Joe's wife did noticed that a Hardee's employee was leaning out of the drive-thru window to get a better view of the aerial phenomenon.

When I asked them to describe the object, Joe said it was a neon green teardrop-shaped object that blended into a bright yellowish toward the front. He also estimated that it was about two houses in length and was completely silent. Joe also noticed that the UFO's tail flashed three rapid sequences of white strobes.

After losing sight of the object, Joe and his wife drove past a Waffle House to a nearby residential neighborhood in the direction where it disappeared. As they drove up Speeks Drive (a dead-end street), Joe and his wife saw residents looking upwards and pointing toward the area where they had also seen the object. Joe also stated that he saw a black sports utility vehicle parked on the side of the road, with a man looking upward. They could not see anything else at that point and drove back home.

As a follow-up, I contacted several businesses that Joe and his wife mentioned during their encounter. On December 1, 2009, I called the local Hardee's and left my contact information with an employee. I called back four days later and spoke with a manager who told me that she had not heard of this event. I called the

Waffle House restaurant on December 1, 2009, and left my contact information but never received a return call from anyone.

Finally, on December 2, 2009, I emailed the Chesterfield County Police Department. I received a reply the following day:

Hello Mr. Gagnon,

I have checked to see if we received any calls for service for UFO sightings on Nov. 27 and we have not discovered any such calls for service under the UFO term. Please note that we receive hundreds of calls for service and callers describe events in various ways. If and when you do speak with your contact, perhaps you can establish if he or she indeed contacted our Emergency Communications Center.
Best Regards,
(Name withheld)
Public Information Coordinator
Chesterfield County Police Department

On December 4, 2009, I contacted the Manchester Volunteer Rescue Squad and spoke with Bill. He said that the dispatch log for that day only showed a gas leak at a nearby Lowe's store and nothing at all associated with aerial phenomena. An email that I sent to *The Richmond Times-Dispatch* newspaper on December 4, 2009, but received no reply.

CONCLUSION:

The anomaly that Joe described was not unique. A nearly identical unidentified aerial phenomenon was witnessed two years earlier in Charlotte, North Carolina, on January 23, 2007. An internet search revealed a January 24, 2007 article of a UFO sighting from *The Charlotte Observer* newspaper; around 8:00 p.m., a J. Neal witnessed what he described as a bright blue-green object with a white tail that also had flashing and strobing lights, just as in Joe's account.

Chapter Three: Christopher Bledsoe Abduction Case

This challenging case consists of many perplexing events that involved four adults and one teenager that took place in Hope Mills, North Carolina on the evening of January 8, 2007. The main witness of these events was Christopher L. Bledsoe, Sr., who is a licensed commercial pilot and home builder. With him was one of his sons who confirmed that the following events had indeed taken place in a remote forest near Cape Fear River.

The phenomena that started on January 8, 2007, did not just occur to Christopher. A few weeks later his wife reluctantly revealed to him that she had seen frightening 'shadow people' drift inside their home. This provided confirmation to Christopher that the events he experienced had 'spilled' over into his home. Following these sightings, Christopher and his family suffered great distress and isolation for many months. Today after fourteen years, he and his family still experience some reverberations from his otherworldly encounters, although it has become somewhat less invasive than it once had been.

On October 10, 2007, Christopher felt it was time to file an official report with Mutual UFO Network. Soon after MUFON received his report, Deputy Director of Investigations Jim DeManche called Christopher and asked him if he could send a regional investigator to his home for an interview. Christopher felt that the on-site investigation should be scheduled at a much later date. After a few phone calls were exchanged with local North Carolina MUFON Field Investigator Steve McGee, the first on-site meeting took place in January 2008.

At the time Christopher filed the report, he was suffering from a serious health condition. However, he felt that he needed to divulge his nightmarish experience to investigators who may have a better understanding of what had occurred.

Christopher's indecision to report the events to MUFON soon after the incident may have also caused some potential trace evidence to be lost due to inclement weather, season changes, foot traffic, and lawn management. Nonetheless, I was fortunate enough to photograph some physical signs that remained in his backyard during my investigation. I was also able to find lawn scorching images that had been captured by Google satellite imagery at that time.

Steve McGee's initial report was submitted to the MUFON CMS (Case Management System) database. Shortly thereafter, McGee had to temporarily withdraw from being the case investigator due to important family obligations. In McGee's absence, I was selected as the lead investigator to this incredible case as a STAR FI.

I received the case file in February 2008 that included a great deal of information about Christopher. I learned that he was a successful home builder, had a commercial pilot's license, had several awards and certificates of merit, and was active in church and school functions. Overall, it appeared that Christopher was a well-respected member of his community of Hope Mills.

I was deployed by MUFON International Director James Carrion as a STAR Team Investigator to continue the investigation of Christopher Bledsoe, Sr., and his son. Here is part of an email I sent to both James Carrion and Deputy Director of Investigations Jim DeManche on Feb 13, 2008, shortly before I departed to North Carolina.

> "Many months have gone by and the potential trace may have been altered by the elements. Just to be safe, I suggest bringing a Geiger counter, an EMF meter, and a GPS receiver. I will also seek for a potential landing site...I have molding plaster in my field case along with plastic bags, containers, and related tools."

During my first on-site investigation on the Bledsoe Case, I identified a key piece of information that changed the course of the entire investigation. Interviews with Christopher, I learned that he experienced a period of missing time, which elevated this case to a

Close Encounter of the Fourth Kind (CE4).

Countless emails were exchanged between MUFON team members that were part of this case, including Deputy Director J. DeManche, Director J. Carrion, and Board of Directors member Chuck Reever. On April 14, 2008, I shared my suspicions about Christopher's account of missing time, which was indicative of a potential alien abduction. Later that evening I received a follow-up email from Steve McGee that read that Christopher Sr. had agreed to undergo hypnosis to try to recover the missing time.

MUFON Case: 8103
Location: Hope Mills, NC, Cumberland County
Date: February 23-24, 2008
Investigator: Norman Gagnon – STAR Field Investigator

Christopher Bledsoe, Sr. River Encounter

I first met Christopher Bledsoe Sr. at a Kangaroo Express gas station for a quick coffee break at 09:23 am. From there, I followed him to his residence, which was a house built in 2006 on three acres of land not far from town. As Christopher and I walked into his backyard, I was greeted by his Chesapeake Bay retriever Rose and shortly after by his teen son Chris, hereafter identified as Junior. At this time, Christopher began to share his ominous experience that began at the Cape Fear River.

Christopher Sr. with his son Jr. Norman Gagnon © 2008

On January 8, 2007, at approximately 2:30 p.m.
Christopher, his 17-year-old son Junior and three of Christopher's
subcontractor friends, (David M., Donnie A., and Gene R.) were
fishing along the river's edge. After about two hours, Christopher
felt he needed to be alone for a while so he took a walk. He left the
river and walked past his Crew Cab pickup truck and the glow of
the camp's fire pit onto the road. He continued up a muddy
pathway bordered on either side with trees and thick vegetation.

As he paced forward, Christopher suddenly heard rustling leaves and crackling branches on his left side; he had a strange feeling that he was being followed. He was certain that it was not his son or friends, and any nearby wildlife would have been frightened away. Whatever presence this was made Christopher feel very uncomfortable.

Christopher continued to walk up and a few minutes later he was just about to leave the trail to an open field near Horse Trail Road. Still feeling that he was being shadowed, then Christopher's attention was drawn toward the sky. Facing west, Christopher saw two bright orange orbs that hovered motionless about 1000 feet from him near the intersection of Horse Trail Road and Marsh Road.

Christopher described the orbs as dual-setting suns surrounded by what appeared to be swirling flames. Feeling uneasy with what he was witnessing, Christopher turned around to dart back to the river toward his companions but stopped when he observed something else above him to his right. The sky "opened" to reveal what he called an 'interdimensional doorway'. In disbelief, Christopher watched as a third orange orb swiftly flew out of it and joined the other two objects. They floated silently above the background of trees. This unsettled Christopher and he immediately crouched down near the shrubbery to inch away in order to not be seen by these fiery anomalies.

Soon, Christopher found himself running back down the path in the darkness as he was careful not to stumble as he headed back toward the camp. Christopher soon joined with his friends that were waiting near the river. As he caught his breath from running, Christopher realized that his son was not with his friends. In a panic, Christopher returned to the woods and called his son's name. Shortly afterward, Junior soon emerged from the bushes, shaken and terrified.

Junior's River Encounter

At the time his father was away to the open field above, Christopher's 17-year-old son Junior placed his fishing pole down and also went for a walk to stretch his legs. As Junior wandered a few yards toward the forest's edge, he pushed aside a few shrubs and continued roaming the area looking for deer. After a while, one of Christopher's friends realized that he had been gone for a long time. Concerned, Donny went to the Crew Cab truck and drove up to Horse Trail Road to find Christopher. With still no sign of Christopher, Donny drove to the entrance of March Road. He turned around and slowly returned to camp all the while looking on in the field for any sign of Christopher. Unsuccessful, Donny turned on his headlights and returned to camp near the river. By this time, Christopher had been missing several hours.

During this time period, Junior wandered the woods and noticed two glowing red lights a few yards away hovering a couple feet near the base of the tree trunks. A moment later, Junior lost sight of them and his attention was drawn near the area where he heard the rustling of foliage. He then saw two obscured creatures scurrying out of the forest and toward an open area above the riverbank. Junior froze in his tracks and slowly squatted down to hide behind the undergrowth. He watched the creatures walk near a trash barrel as if they were looking for something. One picked up an empty bottle and closely examined it. The other was motionless and slowly turned its head directly toward Junior's hiding place. At this point, Junior realized that he was unable to move.

River Humanoids Description

During my interview, Junior first described them as "creatures". Junior told me that while he was hidden, he described them as two small humanoids between three and four feet tall. Both were wearing what appeared to be glowing red goggles that had a type of flashing or scanning light between the lenses.

Junior tried to make sense out of what he was seeing when the humanoids were suddenly illuminated by the headlights of the returning Crew Cab truck. He watched as the humanoids were startled and then unexpectedly altered their forms to 'phase' into the surrounding woodlands. Although Junior could no longer see the humanoids, the red lenses from their goggles remained visible as they fled quickly back into the forest.

Junior was petrified of what he just witnessed but decided to stay hidden because he knew the creatures were close by. Junior felt like he had been hiding in the trees for about two hours and was relieved when he heard his father calling his name. Still terrified, Junior quickly ran out to join his father. As Junior regained his voice, he hysterically tried to describe his encounter. He also shouted to his father, "Where were you, Dad!?"

Junior and his father returned pass the fire pit together and met up with their friends near the river's edge. Once there, Christopher and Junior interrupted each other several times trying to describe what they had just seen. Their friends did not know how to react and appeared baffled by what they were told.

At this point, Christopher's friend Donny noticed several bright stars wavering above them. He pointed and shouted, "Look up!" All five of them looked up and noticed eight lights moving erratically in the distance. Three of the lights separated from the formation and plummeted down toward the river and came to rest over the trees. Each object's intensity diminished as their colors changed from a bright white to an orange color and all began to then pulsate. Still pulsing, the lights rose and shifted slightly away from the terrified group, who watched as the objects descended slowly and disappear behind the tree line on the far side of the river.

In a panic, they all ran towards the Crew Cab to escape. In the rush, they left behind all of their belongings, including their expensive fishing gear. All of the men shouted as the truck's doors slammed shut. The truck sped up the muddy road and towards the open field. Junior looked through the rear window and saw that the two humanoids he had seen before were behind them. He said that they were both on all fours sprinting like hellish dogs as their glowing red eyes erratically bounced in the dark as they chased after the truck!

When the truck sped off the dirt road onto Horse Tail Road, Christopher abruptly slammed on the brakes. Blocking the road ahead of them hovered a brilliant white ellipse-shaped object about the size of a bus. Christopher said the object appeared to have 'spikes' around it. These protrusions slowly rotated around the object's circumference in a random clockwise and counterclockwise manner, resembling a glowing sea urchin. Their only path to safety was now blocked!

Spiked UFO Illustration by Norman Gagnon © 2020

Christopher noticed a mobile home a few yards away to his right. He rushed there to see if anybody was there. He wanted to find other witnesses to this unbelievable experience. When Christopher approached the trailer, he looked through the window and saw that the inside lights and television were on but nobody appeared to be home. Christopher returned to the truck and blew the horn to get their attention. Suddenly, everybody heard three loud gunshots at a distance. After the shots were fired, the spiked UFO rotated slightly and began to hover near them. As it came toward the Crew Cab, Christopher observed that the spikes had disappeared. The now smooth ellipse-shaped craft lifted into the air and flew away at an incredible rate of speed.

One of the men in the truck shouted, "Christopher, take us home!" The Crew Cab sprayed gravel as it took off as fast as possible across the field that led directly to Marsh Road. They had just escaped what must have felt like an alien invasion. As Christopher sped away to take his friends home, they all continued to see strange lights in the sky that appeared to follow them from a distance. After Christopher dropped off his friends, he decided to take the long way home via Highway 87. As Christopher and his son hurried back home, they noticed a few cars were pulled over to the side of the road. They saw several people standing outside their vehicles looking up at the unidentified lights that hovered in the sky above the area.

Cape Fear River Investigation

The first day of my investigation into the Bledsoe case was February 23, 2008. I met with Christopher and his son and we retraced their steps from Cape Fear River to the top of Horse Trail Road. Something did not feel right and I needed Christopher to verify something for me. I asked Christopher to confirm how long his hike was from the time he left his friends at the river's edge until he returned. He paused for a few seconds and replied that it took about twenty minutes or so. Junior immediately replied, 'Dad, you were gone for over four hours!"

I observed Christopher's facial expression at what his son had just hollered. Christopher closed his eyes in deep thought as if he were struggling to remember what exactly happened during that terrifying night. Christopher admitted that he felt that there may have been more to the river encounter than he remembered. However, when Christopher tried to recall what had happened on top of the hill, he always suffered a headache. I took note of this and wrote down in my field notebook 'Possible missing time'.

The three of us returned to Christopher's house and parked the car. We walked around the right side of the house and toward the backyard and into the trail that led to his dog kennel a few yards away. Christopher continued with his account of what happened after he dropped his friends off at their homes later that night.

After Christopher and his son returned to their empty house, both were understandably very traumatized. Junior ran through the house and made certain that all the doors and windows were locked before pulling down the window blinds and turning on all the lights. They calmed down for a while until around 2:00 a.m. when they felt a vibrational pulse followed by a loud sound as if something large had flown over the house.

Christopher reluctantly stepped outside to investigate but could not find anything out of the ordinary. About forty minutes after the strange noise, all fifteen of his dogs in his kennel began to furiously howl and bark. Their family Chesapeake Bay retriever

Rose also joined in the commotion. He opened the rear door and Rose took off from the patio and ran into the darkness towards the kennel. Junior and Christopher ran outside and followed Rose down the trail toward the kennel to investigate the cause of the turmoil. When they got to the kennel, Christopher and Junior noticed that all of the dogs were facing westward toward the woods at the edge of the backyard. Rose also faced in that direction with her hair bristling on her back. Christopher gave the command "Get them Rose!" She took off through the thick woods towards the rear of the property.

Junior returned to the house and Christopher rushed the opposite way towards the clearing of his backyard near a group of blueberry bushes. He sprang back into the woods in an effort to cut off what Rose was chasing. He came to a large oak tree and paused to catch his breath. There, he came face to face with what he referred to as an 'entity'! He stood there paralyzed just a few feet from a small glowing humanoid. Not knowing what else to do, Christopher said to himself, "You got me...I surrender."

A few seconds later Rose jumped through the brush and landed in the opened area next to Christopher. As Rose bounced back up to face the entity, it immediately disappeared!

During my interview, I asked Christopher to describe the creature in detail. He described it as a child-like humanoid that was about four feet tall. It had a human-like head without a neck connecting it to the torso. The creature's head had goggles with glowing red lenses that were identical to what his son witnessed during his own terrifying experience near the river. The entity appeared to wear a mouthpiece that resembled a breathing apparatus. The upper part of the humanoid's torso had a triangular-shaped overlay or emblem on its chest. The arms were straight and stayed close to its side, but the remainder of the body was difficult to see. Christopher added that the creature's entire body was motionless and appeared to be covered with a clear, shiny glass-like energy field that contoured closely to its body.

Emotionally shaken and exhausted but feeling less anxious that during his earlier experiences at the river, Christopher hurried back to the house but did not tell his son about what he had just seen. He entered the back door and met his son in the family room and sat to tried to calm down a bit. Christopher had a strong craving for a cigarette although he had quit several years ago. He went to one of the rooms and opened the window. He picked up his wife's pack of cigarettes and lit one. As he blew the smoke through the window screen, he was shocked to see a very tall, pale being standing in the side yard about twenty feet from the house staring directly at him. Christopher noticed that after they made eye contact, the creature began to walk toward him.

That was it! Christopher and his son ran out the front door

and got into the Crew Cab. They sped down the road and drove about eight miles. He saw an open hay field and abruptly left the road and drove to the center of it. Christopher turned off his engine and headlights and locked the doors, where they remained until sunrise.

Above is an actual daylight photo of his backyard taken during my first day's investigation where the entity appeared. I superimposed an illustration of the entity depicting its approximate size and location. Photo by Norman Gagnon © 2008

Investigation results of Bledsoe's backyard

After Christopher told me of his experience, I asked Christopher if he found any strange markings, cuts, or puncture wounds on his body after his ordeal.

He said he did not. I began my investigation in his backyard. I noticed that the lawn had a sizable circular pale-brown impression approximately sixteen feet in diameter that appeared to be scorched. In the center of this seared ring was a 48-inch circular patch of greenish grass that was barely affected. Several questions entered my mind, but the most pressing question was, *"Did something land there?"* Upon further investigation, I found other elongated "burnt trails" that weaved throughout his backyard.

Circular impression in the backyard. Photo by Norman Gagnon © 2008

Grass and soil samples from the area were collected within the singed 'landing site' along with control samples from outside this zone. I also used Google Maps' satellite imagery at that time period to view over his property and these pale lawn markings were indeed visible. Photographs of the lawn patterns were also taken as part of my investigation.

Each piece of evidence collected from Christopher's backyard (soil samples and branch lichen) was bagged, tagged, and sealed separately and first shipped to Deputy Director of Investigations J. DeManche. On March 8, 2008, DeManche emailed the team to inform us that he looked over the collected samples and then he expressed mailed the evidence to MUFON headquarters in Fort Collins, Colorado. I also conducted a complete environmental reading around the Cape Fear River where the other incidences took place. However, no unusual readings were detected.

I walked further back into his yard where Christopher came face to face with the entity. I scanned the area where the humanoid stood in front of a large oak tree and to the right of a small stack of bricks. There were no hot spots detected by the TriField Electro-magnetic Detector and just normal background noise from the Geiger counter readings.

Scanning the exact spot where the entity stood. The still
video image from Creative Differences Productions -
Discovery Channel 2008

I next went to the oak tree near where the manifestation
appeared. There was a large overhanging branch suspended a few
feet above where the entity stood. Oddly, this branch was covered
with bright orange flakes that resembled *xanthoria elgans*, a
lichenized species of fungus. After looking at several other trees in
his yard, I concluded that this was the only branch on
Christopher's property that had this fungus growth.

Branch directly above the entity's appearance, covered with orange lichen.
Photo by Norman Gagnon © 2008

On May 13th, 2008, I sent an email to fellow UFO researcher Ted R. Phillips, the Executive Director at the Center for Physical Trace Research (CPTR) of Reeds Spring, Missouri, for some insight on this abnormal growth. This is the question I wrote to Phillips in part:

STI Gagnon: *"This may be a coincidence but could fungi growth on this branch have been produced by the entity's "force field" or by an unknown radiation emitted by it, caused an accelerated growth of this organic matter?"*

Phillip's email reply: *"Norman, yes, not often but I have seen accelerated growth like this, generally mushroom growth. There certainly could be a connection – leaving no stone unturned, it would be worth checking."*

A copy of my MUFON field report was sent to Phillips and was issued a CPTR Trace/Landing Case No. 3,396. Since 1969, T. R. Phillips has worked on several cases with the late Dr. J. Allen Hynek that involved UFO landings with related residual traces that had been collected and analyzed.

On February 24, 2008, the second day of my investigation, I visited Gray's Creek Airport/Cape Fear Aviation in Fayetteville, which was located about a mile and a half from the Cape Fear River encounter site. Airport attendants told me that they had not heard of any unusual lights in the sky or any abnormal activity at all from any of the pilots during the time of the sightings. However, they were familiar with Christopher's strange experience. I also emailed both the North Carolina U.S. Army Fort Bragg and Pope Air Force Base, both of which are approximately fifteen miles from the site of Christopher's sightings. Specifically, requesting about any reports or phone calls pertaining to strange anomalies that were seen above the area on the night of January 8, 2007. My inquiries were soon followed by an elaborate symphony of chirping crickets. Neither base replied to my emails.

My notification to the MUFON team informing them that the investigation had been elevated to a possible Close Encounter of the Fourth Kind caused a ripple effect of sorts. Ultimately this finding made headlines within the ufology community and attracted the attention of Hollywood. Word of the Bledsoe encounter also revitalized the MUFON North Carolina chapter.

This encounter encouraged MUFON Director James Carrion to establish a new Chief Investigator position for the state, which was filled by MUFON Field Investigator Richard Lang.

On May 23, 2008, I sent an email to our unit suggesting that David, Donnie, and Gene (the three fishermen) be interviewed individually with their accounts videotaped. The team concurred with the request. During this time, field investigator Steve McGee returned from his hiatus and joined Richard Lang to gather additional information from the three men. McGee and Lang were also asked to contact a psychologist and other related specialists during the preproduction of the first episode of The Discovery Channel's series *UFOs Over Earth*. This episode was filmed between June 18 and June 20, 2008.

Christopher Bledsoe Hypnotic Regression.

About five months after my investigation Lang's team scheduled an appointment with psychologist Dr. Michael O'Connell on July 14, 2008. Dr. O'Connell agreed to conduct a hypnosis session with Christopher to determine if he could recollect what happened during his missing time. Christopher gave his consent to be hypnotized and the entire session was videotaped. Although I haven't seen this video in its entirety, I believe that Christopher may have experienced his abduction near the top of the hill at Horse Trail Road after he witnessed the three orange orbs. Under hypnosis, Christopher described some details about the inside of the craft. He said that he was in a circular room with lights all around him and that there was a sort of pedestal that he believed to be the main console of this craft. Christopher went into detail about the occupants of the craft. He noted that there were two very tall and skinny aliens he called 'guardians' and a number of smaller entities that he described as their 'children'.

On the first day of the shoot, I met with fellow team investigators at the Double Tree Hotel in Fayetteville, North Carolina. There I was introduced to a few members of the show's production crew and retired FBI Special Agent Robert J. Drdak (the polygraph examiner chosen specifically for the case).

After leaving the hotel, my first task at hand was to visit local law enforcement agencies to determine if there were any records of unusual aerial anomalies from the night of January 8, 2007. Both the Sheriff's Office in Fayetteville and the Hope Mills Police Department had no records of "strange lights in the sky." The Fayetteville Sheriff's Office watch commander told me that if there were any unusual sightings from that night, he would have certainly remembered that. After leaving the Sheriff's Office, I drove back to Christopher's home to join the production crew. I was later filmed interviewing Christopher and his son Junior in the dining room. As they described the entities, I made composite drawings of what they had witnessed at both sites.

On the final day of the shoot, I sat in my car with the director, cameraman, and boom operator. The production crew was huddled in the back seat filming me in the front seat placing a phone call to the local newspaper, *The Fayette Observer*. I asked an employee if they could search their newspaper's archives for articles with the keywords of 'UFOs', 'strange lights', 'aerial phenomena', 'meteor and satellite'. Unfortunately, their search revealed that there were no reports in their database with these headlines.

Months later during the TV viewing of the series premiere episode on Discovery Channel, I saw to my surprise that the production kept my car footage in the show! Most of my scenes from my three days' video shoots ended up on the cutting-room floor as they say since the episode had to fit within a 40-minute time frame.

There were many criticisms from the viewers of this episode pertaining to the results of the polygraph test that was given to Christopher and how it was interpreted by Mr. Drdak. Although I do understand why the polygraph test was used in this case, I did not totally agree with the opinion of the examiner. Christopher has experienced terrifying encounters with otherworldly humanoids and related aerial manifestations that lasted more than ten hours, then having him be connected to this machine and asked the question, *"Did you come in contact with an alien?"* The typical physiological responses to this question would most certainly induce strong physical and emotional reactions from anyone who had gone through this traumatic ordeal, resulting in intense fluctuation signals on the polygraph.

'UFOs Over Earth - The Fayetteville Incident' episode can be viewed through the Discovery + and highlights from the episode can also be viewed on YouTube.

Shortly after the episode aired, a few people from the Fayetteville area came forward and contacted Christopher to let him know that they have also seen unexplained lights on that fateful night. However, they were not the only people who were interested in Christopher's account. From my investigation in 2008 on, government officials, independent researchers, and curiosity seekers have all visited Christopher Bledsoe, Sr. to speak with him and more significantly, to stroll in his backyard where some of these mysterious events took place. Even officials from To the Stars Academy of Arts & Science (TTSA) have contacted him. Christopher, you have many believers out there my friend.

Christopher reported that since the 2007 abduction, he has continued to experience anomalous events. Apart from the bright spheres and related anomalies that occurred near the river and at his home that night, he has continued to experience events on his property. In October 2012 a northern catalpa tree in his backyard spontaneously burst into flames on three separate occasions within a few hours' time, even after being hosed down with water between each fire. He said that the tree's flames came from its hollowed-out crevice that happened to be facing toward the circular landing impression approximately twelve feet away. As for the oak branch covered with the orange lichen, I discovered in the backyard four years prior, this same untouched tree deteriorated and left behind a decayed stump only a few feet high. Did a mysterious energy emanate from the entity accelerate the tree's natural lifespan until it crumbled and fell over?

In addition to the backyard tree mysteriously catching fire, Christopher Bledsoe has continued to see strange glowing lights and orbs hover above his property. His later encounters were different from the 2007 sightings, but they were nonetheless awe-inspiring events. He also witnessed an appearance of an angelic-like being that he described as the 'Shining Lady'. Unlike Christopher's confrontations with the other beings, this visitor was much less frightening and actually gave him a sense of wellbeing. He also said that these recent appearances have seemed to be more spiritual to him today rather than the nuts-and-bolts space crafts with their ominous occupants trying to restrain him.

In the winter of 2016, the Bledsoe family moved out from this property and into a new home (or cabin as he calls it) next to a beautiful pond. His closest neighbors are jovial ducks and geese. However, it seems that the Bledsoe family were followed by these anomalies but now they appear to remain at a non-threatening distance.

I visited Christopher in March of 2018 to see how his family is doing, a ten-year reunion of sorts since I first met him during my 2008 investigation. I was also introduced to the newest members of the family…newly hatched goslings. During my visit and after our lunch, I shared with him some of my own paranormal experiences from my life's journey and I told him that it was not by chance that I ended up in his backyard a decade ago. He nodded his head in agreement.

Norman Gagnon with Christopher Bledsoe Sr. © 2018

Hollywood executives along with movie consultant and author Dr. Diana Walsh Pasulka from the University of North Carolina Wilmington, with the Philosophy and Religion Department, have taken interest in Christopher Bledsoe's story regarding the development of a potential drama series based on his 2007 extraterrestrial encounters, of which much more details of his experiences will be revealed. I have been contacted by producers as well, so this should be a very interesting project indeed.

Fade to black.

Chapter Four: Ghost Hunting 201

In 1999, I created a website with the web hosting service of AOL Hometown that highlighted a timeline of the paranormal events that I had investigated and experienced throughout my life. This website was inspired by a 35mm photograph that I took in 1995 on an expedition. It was of a sunrise that peeked above the top of an old church in Mexico. In the photo, there appeared to be a luminous figure that was encircled by an enormous halo hovering above the church's rooftop. (See Chapter 11)

I called my website 'Gagnon's Phenomenons', which I thought was a catchy play on words at the time. After about a year or so, I changed the name and redesigned the page so that it focused on my new team of volunteer paranormal investigators. My group of specialists was called *Supernatural Entity Anomaly Research and Cryptid Hunters* or *SEARCH.* I had a list of local ghost hunters that were available and that included a historian and a physicist that assisted me in my quest to investigate any unearthly sightings.

Supernatural Entity Anomaly Research & Cryptic Hunters,
an acronym and logo I created in 2005 ©

By 2003 ghost hunting and the study of the paranormal was in full swing. There were countless reported haunted sites in my own backyard of Alexandria, Virginia, that needed to be accessed, explored, and investigated. I reached out and contacted a nearby ghost hunting team, the D.C. Metro Area Ghost-watchers (DCMAG) and I met founder and leader Al Tyas. Al and I exchanged theories of ghost hunting, investigation techniques, and had experimented with the latest equipment that was being introduced in the paranormal investigation field at the time.

Al also spoke fondly of his ghost hunter colleagues up north who had investigated haunted locations in and around Rhode Island for almost fifteen years. Their names were Jason Hawes and Grant Wilson of The Atlantic Paranormal Society (TAPS). Al was a big part of the TAPS' extended family.

Al and I talked about the possibility of me doing investigations with DCMAG. He was very selective on who he chose to be on his team, and I had to prove myself to be an adept and competent ghost hunter. The first task at hand was that I needed to earn my merit badge in 'ghostology' of sorts to get the seal of approval from DCMAG. I was asked to participate in a handful of field investigations with fellow ghost-watchers within the Washington D.C. metropolitan area, and one city, in particular, was the historic district of Old Town, Alexandria.

After approximately seven weeks of fieldwork that yielded some startling anomalies on film, Al asked if I wanted to join

DCMAG as a trustee! Of course, I eagerly accepted his invitation and he added me to his contact list. So, after being brought onboard to DCMAG, I became in a way part of TAPS' extended family as well…or perhaps a second cousin once removed.

In the spring of 2004, I received a phone call from Al asking me to join his team on an investigation of a location in Old Town at The Christmas Attic's House in the Country store. We all met in a brick-paved alley next to the store at around 09:30 p.m. then we entered the shop. After our briefing, we broke into individual teams and kept in contact with hand radios. It was one of my most fascinated investigations with Al and his team. Below is my account of the events that we experienced during the investigation.

Christmas Attic's House in the Country-Store
DCMAG Case
(Old Town) 107 N. Fairfax St., Alexandria, VA,
Year built: 1795
March 13, 2004

Norman Gagnon © 2004

The house that we investigated was built in 1795 and was occupied by the Schafer family in the mid-1860s. In June of 1868, a young lady by the name of Laura Schaffer was upstairs preparing for her wedding to Charles Tennesson. As Laura was finishing getting ready for her ceremony, she picked up a kerosene lamp. Unbeknownst to her, the lamp had a small crack in it and kerosene leaked all over her beautiful wedding gown. Frustrated and shocked at what had taken place, she dropped the lit lamp and it shattered on the floor. The flame ignited her kerosene-soaked wedding dressed, which immediately caught fire.

As the flame consumed her dress, Laura panicked and ran down the hall toward the staircase screaming for help. However, Laura's running fed more oxygen to the flames and the fire quickly engulfed her. Laura's mother met her at the base of the steps and tried to extinguish her daughter's wedding dress; however, she received several burns on her arms in the process. The fire was eventually put out, but Laura was severely burned all over her body. Laura died the next day from her injuries. Charles was heartbroken over Laura's death and committed suicide by shooting himself in the head with a revolver a few weeks later. This horrible series of events were covered in the June 29, 1868 edition of *The Alexandria Gazette.*

Since Laura's death, her apparition has been seen in the third-story bedroom where the fire originated as to other parts of this home as well. More frequently, the faint smell of smoke has been detected throughout the house as well. Employees who noticed the smell would often go through the house to make sure that it was not on fire. After The Christmas Attic opened in the store in 1970, several employees have experienced poltergeist activity; countless times they have had to pick up merchandise that had been knocked down from the store's shelves on the first and second floor.

Al had contacted the owners of The Christmas Attic and we were given permission to investigate the house after hours. Arrangements were made and after the store closed for the evening on March 13, 2004, the team of four investigators began to investigate the 209-year-old colonial-style building.

While the other members of DCMAG conducted their own portion of the investigation, I walked through the house taking multiple photographs. In addition to my digital camera, I also had a 35mm camera. I shot three photographs of the lobby staircase from directly across the store's front entrance. One photograph of the staircase depicted a strange lighted anomaly on the carpeted steps. The team analyzed the photo to determine if the camera flash could have caused this variance in the image. However, we determined that it was not caused by a flash reflection or lens flare.

I included the photograph analysis with negative on the next page.

Norman Gagnon © 2004

Here is a copy of the actual 35mm negative and photograph of the stair anomaly. On the left is the original photograph. Right/top is the cropped image that had the brightness and contrast adjusted via Photoshop (notice how there are what appear to be "incandescent particles" surrounding the apparition.) Actual negative bottom right.

This was a very fascinating sliver of evidence from this investigation. Did my camera shutter capture the residual image of Laura Schaffer's horrible accident from 137 years ago? This photo was also utilized in the Travel Channel's *Weird Travels* series via Authentic Entertainment Inc.

120

Fish Market Restaurant

S.E.A.R.C.H. Case

(Old Town) Alexandria, VA

October 22 and November 10th, 2004

One evening in late October 2004, I was walking out of a Springfield, Virginia coffeehouse and was approached by a young man at the entrance. He asked me about my SEARCH embroidered logo on my tactical vest I was wearing. It was full of technical field equipment, including a PVS-7 Night Vision goggle. I explained to him that I was a paranormal researcher and was on my way to investigate an alleged haunted park in nearby Annandale. His eyes grew wide, and he smiled. This guy told me that he was an employee at a seafood restaurant in Old Town that was actively haunted. He said that for years the night managers had experienced ghostly activity in this old building that housed the restaurant. I jotted down the man's contact information and the restaurant's name before I left to investigate the alleged haunted fields. The restaurant sounded like a promising lead.

I called the number he gave me and had a noteworthy telephone conversation with the seafood restaurant's manager, Lisa C. She and her staff agreed to meet with me at the restaurant. That Saturday evening, I walked in the Fish Market Restaurant and sat at the first-floor dining area, and placed my order of the Fisherman's Platter that included the most tender scallops.

While I was eating, the restaurant's bartender came and sat at my table to have a brief chat about a strange incident she experienced. She told me that one night she had just finished closing the first floor's west end bar and was about to walk out the door when she heard the ice dispenser being used. As she went back inside to check out the bar area but no one was there, then a cluster of ice was thrown across the room and shattered against the wall!

Shortly after the bartender left me, another staff member came to my table and shared her own incident involving an empty glass that slid across the bar's counter. This young lady said that she and two other employees had seen an empty glass gently slide across the bar's counter. She hesitantly whispered, "The glass moved by itself a couple of feet or so and there was no one behind the bar. How crazy is that?" She then stood up and walked away from the table.

After my delicious meal and as I was waiting for my doppio espresso to arrive, the assistant manager, 'PC' came to my table and shared his own experience. He told me about a second-floor storage room where the bar's liquor was kept. On a few occasions, the light in the room had been seen to turn on by itself when employees walked past it. This often happened just before the closing time as employees were about to lock up for the night.

He emphasized that this storage did not have a motion sensitive automatic light.

PC also shared with me his own experience that took place just months before. After he closed the restaurant and was about to leave he heard a man, woman, and child talking. He said that it sounded like it was coming from the second floor. He hurried upstairs and found that the dining room was empty. PC then quickly left to attend to some customers.

Before I had finished my meal, four separate employees came to me while I had dinner and told me of their own paranormal experiences that involved poltergeist activity and other manifestations throughout this timeworn structure. I took careful notes and after I went home I began to research the history of the restaurant.

History

The building in which the restaurant is located was built in the heart of Alexandria, Virginia's waterfront district in the eighteenth century. It was part of large groups of warehouses originally built to store cargo from ships that had recently arrived from Europe.

I learned that the restaurant in which I was having dinner had quite a history.

In the 1800s, the warehouse was used as a field hospital during the Civil War. In the 1800s, the warehouse was used as a field hospital during the Civil War. After the war, beef and other meats were cured inside the building. In the early 1900s, it became the site of a soft drink production and bottling business and during Prohibition, another tenant brewed something much more potent. In 1976, Ray Giovannoni bought the vacant depository and converted it into a three-story restaurant with five dining rooms called 'The Fish Market'. The restaurant was sold in 2008 and was entirely renovated, and with a new staff and manager at the helm.

Investigations: October 22nd & November 10th, 2004

After listening to the independent accounts of at least four separate employees, I decided that the restaurant would definitely be worth investigating. I asked a DCMAG member and communication agent Pat H. to join me on both investigations of the historic three-story brick building.

Entrance of the Fish Market Restaurant.
Norman Gagnon © 2004

Prior to the first night's investigation, the night manager PC gave Pat and me a brief tour of the establishment that is just a cobblestone's throw from the western bank of the Potomac River. During the walkthrough, PC pointed to a wall decoration of an old painting of an unknown eighteenth-century naval officer with large epaulets on the shoulders of his uniform.

He began to describe an incident that took place while one night while he was in the process of closing the restaurant. As he walked to the second-story staircase, he noticed that the portrait was no longer on the wall but had been unhooked and levitating about a foot away from the wall. When he realized what he was seeing, the portrait crashed to the floor! At this point, he emphasized that the portrait did not just fall but appeared to have been thrown down with a great force. He also clarified that as the portrait was face down on the floor, he made the observation that the frame wire and to the nail that supported it on the brick wall was both intact.

Portrait that was found levitating. Norman Gagnon © 2004

Based on the paranormal accounts of the employees, the most active part of the restaurant was on the second-floor. Before we started the investigation, Pat and I closed the door to the second floor stairwell to reduce the noise level from the few night shift employees that remained below on the first-floor dining and bar area. We turned off most of the lights on the floor to reduce the chance of having reflections appear in any photographs.

As the investigation began, Pat and I each took a different part of the floor to examine. Pat switched on his EMF meter and began to scan his area while I took photos from the other side of the dining room closest to the balcony doors that led to a couple of exterior dining tables. While I was taking photos, Pat found a door that was propped open. Cautiously he walked through the doorway and found himself in a rather confined space. He carefully proceeded forward until he unexpectedly heard a loud, 'tsweee...swosh!' This was followed by a loud shriek! I immediately shouted from across the room: "Pat, are you okay?" He replied, "Yeah, the f***ing auto-sensor from the urinal activated the flusher!" Remember, be prepared for anything during a ghost hunt.

On both nights of the investigation, I conducted EMF scans throughout the restaurant. As I suspected, I picked up high readings near the staircase on the second floor's east wall near the naval officer's portrait. Although the readings were intriguing, I believe that the elevated spikes were caused by the inner wall's electrical wiring.

Pat also made several attempts to record EVPs. However, on both nights there was simply too much background noise from the first floor. Our second investigation of the restaurant did not reveal anything unusual from our recorders, detectors, or cameras.

After the investigation, I dropped off my 35mm rolls of film at a local film processing center. When I reviewed my printed photos, I apparently photographed two separate, glowing anomalies. The first photograph was taken in the attic and it contained a very bright translucent bluish orb hovering in front of a large dumbwaiter pulley wheel. The second image was of a mysterious red ellipse-shaped form floating above a table near the 2nd-floor dining area's southern wall. I immediately noticed this "red entity" on the photo and I showed it to the technician behind the counter for his opinion. After examining the negative strip for a minute on a lightbox, he said that this anomaly was not caused by the film's chemical processing or by a light leak from the camera case, and it definitely was not a lens flare. As a final point, he said to me, "Whatever this is on the negative, you have captured it within the parameter on this one single 35mm frame."

The actual 35mm photo and negative of the "red entity".
Norman Gagnon © 2004

Richmond Theatre aka Old Town Theater

DCMAG Case

(Old Town) Alexandria, Virginia

August 28, 2004

I joined DCMAG's team on their second investigation in a timeworn theater that was built in the early 1900s. The Old Town Theater opened in 1914 and was well known for being one of the first theaters to show silent movies in the area. When the films were not being shown, the Old Town Theater also hosted several Vaudeville performances. There was a large hardwood dance hall on the second floor until a balcony was added in 1932.

Fast forward to 1980. The inside of the now Old Town Theater had been renovated to include a second movie screen in the upper level. Once the renovations were complete and the movie theater was reopened, the name was changed to Old Town Theaters 1 and 2. Additional renovations were made in 1999 and 2002 that helped to capture the ambiance of the theater's history. A stage for comedy routines, plays, and other live performances was added. Unfortunately, one century after The Old Town Theater opened its doors for the first time, the doors closed on this historical landmark for the last time.

2004 Old Town Theater Investigation

Prior to our first investigation of the theater in 2004, Al Tyas gave us a brief background on the paranormal activity that had been reported by a few employees.

One account centered on a female projectionist who was working alone at the upper-level film booth one evening. Her encounter started when she heard giggling echoing inside the projection booth. A second event she shared was more unnerving. This time, she said she felt being pinched while bending over to pick up a film projector reel off the floor.

This case was actually the second investigation conducted by DCMAG at The Old Town Theater. A few months prior a different DCMAG team had been allowed to investigate the theater. During their investigation, they heard mysterious banging from the projection booth. After carefully examining the area, the investigators were unable to find a source for the sounds. There were also several photographs of the orb(s) taken in one seating area on the balcony. Examination of the photos concluded that they were not caused by specks of dust reflected by camera flashes. Also, a few investigators on the team felt lightheaded on the upper floor. These events indicated that a second investigation of the theater was warranted.

I'm holding a TriField EMF Meter. August 2004

DCMAG team was given carte blanche to fully explore this majestic theater. One could actually smell the history within this century-old structure. I decided to start my investigation by taking multiple 35mm photographs on the first floor close to the stage. While near the left emergency exit door, I heard electronic beeps every few seconds from the second-floor balcony. The sound came from fellow investigator Frank Polievka's TriField Natural EMF Meter. By the number of electronic beeps I heard, it appeared that Frank is detecting something anomalous from the balcony above.

I was curious about what was triggering Frank's meter so I decided to join him on the balcony.

Frank's location was where the orbs were captured on film during the previous investigation. Once there, I said, "Frank, I have an idea. I'd like to take photos of your vicinity at the precise time your meter alarm goes off and perhaps I may catch something on film." Frank agreed. When Frank's TriField alarm sounded, my camera flashed on as photos were taken.

As I continued gauging the other side of the projection booth, I noticed a small hidden latch on the carpeted floor. After taking a closer look, I discovered that there was a concealed trap door. Al and I decided to open it and we discovered that there was a long, dusty, rather unstable ladder that disappeared into the darkness below. This warranted further exploration perhaps on another investigation. At 02:00 AM, we ended our investigation.

The day after the investigation, I went to process my film. My negatives depicted two anomalies. The first photograph was taken from the base of the stage looking upward toward the entrance of the theater. DCMAG investigator, Michael Richards was in the photograph walking down the aisle. This photo depicted a burst of energy that looked to be only a few inches from my face…this was rather discomforting after examining it closely.

A ghostly photobomb?   Norman Gagnon © 2004

The second photograph was one that I had taken when Frank's TriField meter went off. I was able to capture a glowing blue orb that was right above Frank's head. I believe that this anomaly was actually the source that triggered his meter. The photograph revealed the motion streak of the orb as it tried to escape my camera shutter!

Frank Polievka with a TriField Natural EMF Meter. Norman Gagnon © 2004

133

SEARCH Case

Haymarket, Virginia

Year Built: 1790

Multiple on-site investigations

History

This area where the La Grange Winery was built was once a hunting ground for the western Iroquois nations. Later, the property was part of Robert "King" Carter's 1600s Bull Run tract known as "LaGrange." The brick manor house was built in 1790 and sits on a small hill at the base of Bull Run Mountain off of Antioch Road. The property changed ownership numerous times over the past four centuries. In 1827, Benoni E. Harrison, L.L.D. Doctor of Law acquires the La Grange property. In 1869, Mr. Harrison dies at LaGrange when he was 83 years old.

Abandoned La Grange Manor 1933. Source Library of Congress

In December of 2005, a team of investors and wine connoisseurs purchased the historic La Grange land located off Antioch Road. Shortly after, construction took place to renovate this old manor house and other buildings on this property. Renovations took less than a year and the Winery at La Grange was opened in September of 2006. Did the restoration of this dilapidated manor house awaken spirits that once resided there?

Today the property includes nearly eight acres of beautiful open fields. The vineyards produce a Cabernet Sauvignon wine with a distinctive flavor imparted to the special grapes of this locality, a "goût de terroir" unique among this hearty Virginian landscape. They also produce a Chardonnay, Rosé, and a delectable port-style dessert wine.

La Grange Winery today.   Norman Gagnon © 2004

Manor House January 2008

There are so many fascinating areas of the winery's manor house that a person would need to explore to appreciate. A few yards from the winery's rear doorway is a building known as the Barrel Room. This is where the pressing, filtration, and bottling of the wine takes place which houses over 200 active wine barrels.

As you first enter through the front door, you will walk into the former dining room that has become the central point for so many visitors – the Tasting Room. One interesting feature of this lobby is the U-shaped bar in front of an old stone fireplace of which a half-glass of wine is kept on the mantle, in memory of Benoni Harrison.

A staff member shared a story with us that a few years ago after a Christmas party, a clean-up crew accidentally took the glass down from the mantle but did not provide a replacement. As the first employee entered the lobby area the next morning, she heard what sounded like someone behind the bar rustling around the wine glass rack. The rustling was immediately followed by the loud sound of smashing glass. Taken aback as she realized that the mantle glass of wine was no longer there, she quickly replaced a half-filled glass of red wine on the mantle for Mr. Harrison. Then she cleaned up the shattered glass on the floor and replaced the wine glass into the rack.

At the left side of the lobby area and across the Tasting

Room there is a gift shop where people can buy souvenirs, a glass of wine or a bottle. Further back is a kitchen and a staircase that leads to the cellar. The manor rests on the original stone-walled foundation that supports a low-ceilinged basement called the Benoni Lounge that was once a root cellar. Some of the exposed support beams show the century-old marks from the axes that shaped them.

SEARCH's Darla Vasilas contacted Chris Pearmund who owned this land at the time, for a potential paranormal investigation. Mr. Pearmund agreed to meet with Darla for a preliminary on-site interview as he imparted a few interesting folklore relating to ghostly activities that took place in this property. Two instances he shared that specifically transpired within the manor's 2nd and 3rd-floor rooms were nicknamed 'The Candle Room' and 'The Cameo Room'. Below are the accounts:

The Candle Room

From the lobby area, there is a staircase that leads to the second floor parlor that is now known as the Candle Room. History reveals that during the Civil War the Union Army was forced to retreat through the area of Haymarket, Virginia, that would include this property. The daughter of the owner of the farm was playing near the woods and found a wounded Union soldier. She went back in to speak to a slave about her discovery. In secret, they arranged that after sundown, the young girl would put a candle in the window to let the soldier know that a helper was coming out with food, water, and roller bandages.

In recent years, folks are still seeing an eerie glow coming through this window. Mr. Pearmund even shared an event that he witnessed himself while he had electricians working on the manor's electrical wiring. One night as he was leaving the manor and walking to his car, he noticed a dimmed, flickering light through the 2nd-floor parlor room window. The strange thing is, the electrical service panel was shut off on that day! There were staff members who also claim to have seen the ghost of a little girl roaming the second floor.

Then there is also the story of the Christmas tree in the Candle Room that was always found lying on the floor the next morning, no matter what type of sturdy stand they were using to support it. Some have said that the tree was blocking the "candlelight" window and perhaps the spirit of the little girl is still making sure this window is unobstructed for her to place a lit candle on the sill.

The Cameo Room

While the third floor was undergoing renovation in 2005, a carpenter found a piece of cameo jewelry hidden within the base of the fireplace. As he tried to reach for the tiny treasure it mysteriously slipped from his grasp.

He said that he did not drop it but insisted that it was pulled from his reach.

Undeterred by this, he removed a couple of wooden floorboards and tried to reach for the cameo again between the joists. Again, it moved away. His bizarre and impromptu treasure hunt quickly ended as he had to close off the floor to complete the third-floor renovations. The worker shared his encounter with some coworkers. Word spread and eventually this room became known as The Cameo Room. As far as our team knows, the phantom cameo is still hidden under the hardwood floor.

I feel that the La Grange Winery was one of the most active paranormal sites that I have ever investigated. That being said, I want to emphasize that there is no malevolence associated with these manifestations. Several La Grange staff and visitors to the manor have described the activity as 'mischievous'. During our investigations we found this to be the case, especially when we dealt with auditory phenomena. For example, during one investigation the team was on the first-floor Tasting Room when we heard noises in the Candle Room on the second floor above us. As we hurried up the staircase to check out the second level and about 15 minutes or so of noiselessness, we heard the lobby door from below slam shut!

And back downstairs we would go. Events like this were common during each of our investigations at this outlandish manor.

On January 6, 2008, Darla Vasilas also interviewed several staff members about their paranormal encounters. The results of the interviews led to our first investigatory visit to the La Grange six days later. Three other investigations were also conducted in November 2012, April 2013, and February 2014, as these dates were scheduled by the La Grange Winery's general manager at the time, given that they had numerous wine tasting and related special events on their calendar.

SEARCH First Investigation: January 12, 2008

The first exploratory team was comprised of myself, Darla, and her husband Steve, and physicist/system engineer Jeremy C.

After entering the manor, we unpacked our equipment and each took a different area of the house to stake out. Alone in the cellar's Benoni Lounge, I began by taking photographs of the room. Later I was startled by a loud thump from above. What I heard through the beamed ceiling (aka the first floor) was a door from the lobby's Tasting Room open and slam shut. This was immediately followed by heavy footsteps! I did not believe this to be a team member randomly walking around without first notifying all of us through our hand radios.

140

So, I raced upstairs to check the lobby area. Oddly, nobody was in the lobby and both doors were locked. As for the rest of the team, they were sitting quietly in the Candle Room on the second floor; they actually thought I was the one causing the commotion below them, but I clarified to them that we may have a visitor from "the other side" that have joined us this evening. I resumed my solo investigation of the cellar's Benoni Lounge.

After about forty more minutes in the cellar, Darla radioed me from the second floor about an unexplained blaring that she was hearing coming from the third floor. I immediately sprinted to the third floor. There, I heard what Darla had reported. The best I can describe the noise was that it sounded like static intermixed with chaotic music coming from one of the empty offices. I cautiously walked inside the room and found a clock radio on a desk blaring at full volume...the dial was positioned between stations. I turned off the radio and contacted the team to what had happened. For the second time that evening, it appeared that the entire team was being played by ghostly influence. A secretary emailed SEARCH a few days later and wrote that she has no idea why her clock radio alarm was set to go off in the midnight hours. The reports from the staff and witnesses were correct, these ghosts were certainly mischievous!

Later that night about 01:45 AM, our investigation resumed as we gathered in the cellar's Benoni Lounge and I revealed in detail with the team what took place a few hours earlier. Steve decided to try out his custom-built Faraday Cage (a shielded enclosure made from a metallic mesh that is used to block electromagnetic fields that can interfere with recording devices that was kept inside.) He placed his shoebox-size EMF cage on one of the tables with a digital recorder enclosed. After we activated the recorder, we left the cellar unoccupied while we investigated the property outside of the Manor House. Two hours later, Steve returned to the cellar to retrieve the recorder with his cage. When we listened to the cellar recording the next day, we could distinctly hear the chair legs rattle and scrape on the concrete floor!

Benoni Lounge: Digital recorder inside a Faraday Cage on top of the rear table. Please note the tiny glowing "orb" in front of the antique grape-wine press.   Norman Gagnon © 2008

It was interesting to see how that management embraced the idea that the manor was haunted. In March 2008, I received a letter from the management of La Grange complementing the SEARCH team for its investigation. I have added a copy of the letter below:

Scan of the La Grange staff memo/newsletter based on my first SEARCH investigation in 2008. The aol link is no longer valid.

Highlights of our findings from our other 3 investigations of the La Grange Manor:

143

Second Investigation: November 2012

As for Steve and Darla Vasilas, they have branched out to start their own ghost hunting group called 'Paranormal Research Organization for Bothersome Entities' (PROBE), as I was quite busy with my UFO cases with MUFON. As a courtesy, they invited me to join them for the other three investigations at the La Grange Manor.

Almost immediately the paranormal pranks began...the ghosts here loved to josh with our team. As we were all in the Tasting Room prepping for our night's investigation, a tiny picture frame on a small plant stand next to the stairwell tipped over in what I would call in a 'controlled manner'. The way that the picture was positioned, if the tiny table was accidentally bumped into, the frame would have simply fallen onto the floor. However, this was certainly not the case because nobody was standing near the table. The frame looked as if it had simply lifted up and gently dropped down flat. This was witnessed by two team members and by a La Grange employee as well.

As the investigation began, the team first decided to sit quietly in the cellar for about forty-five minutes. Soon, we heard the forceful slamming of a door which was followed by loud footsteps from the floor above us.

This was exactly what I had heard from my first investigation of the winery four years ago. Providentially, we all heard the "grand entrance"

Steve immediately ran to the first floor to look into this commotion and was alarmed to discover the strong stench of cigar smoke coming from the area. He immediately radioed the rest of the team to join him on the first floor. We all right away sprang into action. As we passed through the gift shop we could also smell the cigar smoke! Although the aroma was detected by all of us, there was no visible sign of actual smoke. Was this emission produced by Mr. Benoni's ghostly midnight visitation?

Third Investigation: April 2013

Our third visit to La Grange Winery was just as eventful and exciting as our previous two investigations. It appeared that on this night, the epicenter of the paranormal activity was actually on the second floor's Candle Room. This time with an updated arsenal, we placed a laser pen with a grid pattern on the floor in the second-floor hall; if the beam pattern were to be broken by a semi-invisible 'apparition', this would be captured on the infrared night vision video camcorder.

Sitting quietly in the Candle Room, with a digital recorder and EMF detector next to me on the table.   Photo by Darla Vasilas 2013

Later during the night, we returned to the Candle Room and sat quietly for a half-hour or so. Suddenly, we heard a child's voice that came through Darla's hand radio that only lasted about three seconds. As part of this third outing, we once again placed a digital recorder in the cellar in hopes of capturing recordings of the table or chairs being shuffled about as to our first two investigations. We were fortunate enough to hear not only the sound of the chairs' moving but we also captured an undetermined 'shriek' that sounded as if it was close to the recorder. A day later, the video examination of the second-floor hall did show a disruption of the laser grid projection pattern that coincided with the sound of footsteps in this area.

Fourth Investigation: February 2014

The PROBE team and I visited the winery one last time. We were certainly not disappointed as this was the most active of the four investigations. This time, our team made a few changes to our investigative techniques. We placed a video camera in the basement where we captured digital recordings of moving chairs on three occasions and the unidentified cry. After reviewing the footage a day later, we discovered that the camera gently shook up and down with the sound of a chair scraping the concrete floor as it was recorded. Unlike the other investigations, there was a new sound in the cacophony. The camera recorded the sound of shuffling footsteps and unintelligible whispering of voices in the basement. Although we had heard heavy footsteps on the first-floor lobby during previous investigations, this was the first time we recorded it from the cellar.

A video camera set up in the empty Tasting Room captured the sound of a door closing followed by what sounded like a male voice saying "*wow*". The team members were all on the upper floors sitting quietly.

In addition to the lobby noises, the video camera captured a tiny glowing, yellowish-white light source hovering around near the Tasting Room staircase for a few seconds then quickly disappearing off the camera's range. Being in the middle of the winter season, this was definitely not a firefly.

147

The recorded voices were not limited to being detected in the Candle Room. Steve reported hearing voices coming from the first floor's kitchen area near the gift shop. Two investigators also felt a cold breeze passing between them in the second-floor Candle Room.

When Steve and I went back to the cellar's Benoni Lounge to check on our equipment early the next morning about 02:00 AM. Steve suddenly saw a shadowy figure of an ill-defined face and torso peek around the stairwell before quickly retreating back into the darkness! This apparition scared the living daylights out of him as he almost collapsed! Luckily, I grabbed him and led him to a nearby chair to sit down for a few minutes. This was a good time to call it a night as we radioed the team to gather in the Tasting Room to pack our equipment and exchange notes of what took place during our night's investigation.

The basement's Benoni Lounge was eerily active too as we captured recordings of both heavy footsteps entering the first-floor lobby during the midnight hours and chairs with tables being moved and shifted around. Working hypothesis: could this be a ghostly manifestation agitated with the present time furniture arrangement that is, supernaturally speaking, intruding with the accessibility of the cellar's dried goods of the past?

There is also the spirit of a young girl that seems to be haunting the second floor's parlor room (Candle Room).

Is she still keeping watch to ensure that this one window is kept free from obstructions so she can place her tiny candle on the sill to forewarn the wounded Union soldier?

We believe that we have heard and captured plenty of paranormal evidence with our equipment in this 230-year-old manor. In my view, ghost detecting gears are fine in recording and measuring paranormal activity but often the best method of detecting the echoes of the past is by 'still hunting'; sitting quietly and using our four human senses of sight, sound, smell, and touch (feel).

Chapter 5: Ireland Expedition with DCMAG

In the summer of 2006, the founder of D.C. Metro Area Ghost-watchers' Al Tyas asked me if I would be interested in joining his team in Ireland for some exploration and to take on a few ghost hunts at three different ancient castles for a week. I told him that I needed some time to think about it. Five seconds later, I replied with a, "Where do I sign!?"

November 9/10, 2006
(Ireland 5 hours ahead)
Boston Logan International Airport

Under time constraints, I wolfed down my airport's blue-plate special of an undercooked mushroom Swiss burger and warm greasy fries. Then we all rushed to the international terminal to catch our Irish Aer Lingus flight. We arrived at our gate just in time. About an hour after we were airborne, I unwittingly became one liter lighter after losing my lunch partway over the Atlantic Ocean, so I was relieved to land on terra firma again in Dublin International Airport. My tactical watch was set forward five hours as we collected our bags and we soon met with our fellow Irish correspondent and paranormal tour guide Barry Fitzgerald as he received us with a grand smile and firm handshakes.

For D.C. Metro Area Ghost-watchers lead Al, this was his second tour of duty to the Emerald Isle. It included Michael

Richards (USPS Rural Carrier and team *sensitive*), and for the rest of the lineup, all being our first time overseas investigating haunted strongholds. There was the assistant lead Frank Polievka (Senior Firearm Instructor) and his friend Thomas Doughty (Patent Examiner), Ross Foniri (Geologist), along with Jonathan Ness and Lew M, both serving as police officers within the Washington D.C. metropolitan area. This was the beginning of an awesome excursion.

We tossed our gears in the back of Barry's 'Shrouded Steps' passenger tour van and he drove us northwest through the beautiful countryside for nearly 100 kilometers to our first destination, Ross Castle. We have scheduled to stay there for a few nights before moving on to other ghostly destinations in Ireland. Each castle and historic location we visited had such an awe-inspiring history that literally dozens of articles and books have been written about them. However, I will go over each site's general history and then focus primarily on the preternatural elements of each of our inquiries.

Ross Castle, Mountnugent, County Meath
Friday, November 10, 2006

The caretaker of Ross Castle was an Irish gentleman who was more than eager to tell us about the castle's ghostly history. He said that over the years several innkeepers have claimed that the stronghold is haunted by at least one rather unruly spirit. When we asked about what was commonly encountered, and he said that the castle has a reputation of having haunted activity such as the sound of a woman weeping, phantom footsteps, doors opening and closing by themselves, and unexplained shadows.

Norman Gagnon © 2006

History

Back in 1536, Richard Nugent the 11th Lord of Delvin built the castle referred to today as Ross Castle, on the top of a hill close the shore of Lough Sheelin (lake). Lord Nugent had a beautiful daughter named Sabina who enjoyed taking long walks to the outer edge of her father's property near the lake. On one of her many extended strolls, she met a handsome young man and they engaged in a long and meaningful conversation but Sabina was astonished to find out that this young man's name was Orwin O'Reilly, the son of an Irish chieftain and her father's adversary. After a few of these meetings, they fell deeply in love with one another.

Her father later discovered that Sabina had these secret rendezvous with the young O'Reilly and these forbidden gatherings were immediately halted. Broken-hearted, they decided to run away with each other. One windy evening close to sunset, they met near the Lough Sheelin shore and boarded a boat as Orwin started to row across the lake as fast as he could. Unexpectedly, a storm blew in as the waves grew in size and suddenly their small boat was overturned!

Orwin lost the battle and drowned but Sabina was found unconscious atop the overturned boat as she did not wake up for three days. Upon realizing that her lover was gone forever, Sabina sank into deep despair and she locked herself up in the castle's tower and did not eat or drink for many days and with her already weakened condition, she finally fell into a deep sleep from which she never woke up. Many believed that since Sabina's passing, she haunts Ross Castle.

From the main entrance, we walked through the castle's contemporary addition into the open dining area that had a long rustic wooden table next to an antique bookshelf on the left. A few steps on the right of the dining room was an elegantly furnished sitting room with a large stone fireplace. The long hall on the right past the kitchen led us to three ornate bedrooms. At the opposite end of this hallway was the entrance to the original stone tower. I pushed opened the wooden door and climbed the spiral staircase that guided me to three grand bedrooms, each on separate levels of the castle's primal turret. Each chamber was slightly illuminated by the sun shining through the castle's thin vertical arrowslits.

I stayed by myself in the Yellow Bedroom which is in the far northeast wing on the ground floor that has a window with the view facing the Lough Sheelin lake. After unpacking, I laid down for a few hours to rest from my extended flight. After I woke up, my colleagues and I reconvened in the sitting room to prepare for an evening tour of this ancient bastion. While reposing on a sofa, I noticed the affable scent of peat briquettes burning in the fireplace, which added to the ambiance of this enchanting sitting room.

At sundown, our team conducted an outdoor parameter walkthrough and was accompanied by a few pipistrelle bats that circled the tower overhead – at no extra cost. Most of the old stone outer wall and the entrance to the inner courtyard are still standing after nearly six centuries. There is also a remnant of Ross Castle's original medieval chapel wall that is part of this stone fortification, which still bears one small gothic window opening that reveals the rural vista of the distant hills.

After Frank videotaped us exploring the castle's acreage, we all retired to our rustic chambers. I laid in bed for a while and found that it took longer than expected for me to fall asleep. I later heard what I thought was a woman sobbing outside of my bedroom window, and I did not have the iron will to get up and slide the curtains open to have a look-see. I got thinking about how Sabina died of a broken heart over 450 years ago, and this notion did not lessen my heightened situational awareness. However, I finally dozed off but I was awakened a few times during the night by a gentle tapping coming from the hallway. I carefully listened and strangely, it sounded like somebody was beating on a stretched animal skin drum.

The next morning after a hardy Irish breakfast that included black pudding (blood sausage) and bold coffee served in a French-Press. Barry shared with us that near the shore of Lough Sheelin below there are traces of what was once a secret pathway that may have led to an underground grotto that linked to the castle above. After our morning feast, we all walked down the hill and surveyed this site near the lake and we did found several half-buried stones blocks covered with green moss and crawling vines. I would have loved to take part in an archaeology dig of this area for sure!

Saturday, November 11, 2006
Fore Abbey, County Westmeath

We returned to our rooms to pack our cameras and a hand full of euro banknotes. Soon we were on the road being driven south toward County Westmeath, as I was noticing Barry hailing fellow passerby with quick hand waves while still holding to the steering wheel with his thumb. I finally got used to seeing Barry driving from the right side of the vehicle.

Along the way, we made a quick stop to a deserted graveyard we spotted on a hill to examine ancient headstones and Celtic crosses. Next to the graves stood a long-abandoned derelict stone structure without a roof. After an hour, we left the cemetery as we continued for a few more kilometers to the village of Fore to explore the Thirteenth Century Fore Abbey. The abbey ruins are located in a valley north of Lough Lene in County Westmeath. This monastery was founded by Saint Feichin in 660. Since that time, the abbey has been attacked by invaders and rebuilt at least twelve times between the years 771 and 1169. The remains of Fore Abbey that I visited were from its most recent reconstruction in the 13th century.

Fore Abbey Monastery   Photo by Frank Polievka © 2006

After surveying this ancient priory, we roamed the surrounding area and came upon the mystic St. Féichín's Spring where I was able to collect and seal a tiny bottle of this water from the crystal-clear stream. According to local legend, the water from this spring cannot boil and has been used for centuries for its curative properties.

We returned to the abbey for an arranged meeting with regional Wiccans Janet Farrar and Gavin Bone who joined us inside the monastery to tell us a bit of history regarding the abbey from their modern pagan perspective. They also shared with the team tales from local Celtic folklore.

Once we left Janet and Gavin at Fore Abbey, we drove westward toward the agricultural town of Mullingar for a hearty lunch at the Druid's Chair Pub, which was established in 1609. Afterward, some of the team members made a stop at a local grocery store to acquire some spirits for the cold nights ahead.

Our next stop was Donore in County Meath where we explored the megalithic mounds of the Loughcrew Cairns, also known as the "Mountain of the Witch". The mountain trail to the monolith took us nearly a thousand feet above the rural area to first examine a large, altered boulder called The Hag's Chair that measured about 10 feet across, 6 feet high, and is estimated to weigh about 10 tons. As the name implies, this chair-shape monolith was carved out of a single large stone around 3500 BC, resembling a primal throne. It was one of the kerbstones that aligned the circular base of the common tomb at the northern position. Upon closer inspection, the chair has a small cross chiseled onto the surface of the seat.

The largest monolith at the Mountain of the Witch is known as the Cairn T. It is approximately 120 feet in diameter and the entrance to the stone antechamber. The hall leads to a series of Neolithic stones engraved with eccentric carvings that have defied translation for centuries. During the equinoxes' alignment, light from the rising sun shines through Cairn's doorway to illuminate the 'solar petroglyphs' located at the recessed wall on the western end of the chamber.

158

Prior to our hike back down the sacred mountain, I paused for a minute and beheld the spectacular view of the Irish hillsides below and I took a deep breath from the cool North Atlantic air as I also sensed my frontier-duster coat flailing in the wind, which felt phenomenal!

Back at Ross Castle, we prepared for a more systematic night's investigation. The clicking of multiple digital shutters could be heard reverberating throughout the castle. Our Wiccan contacts Janet and Gavin also joined us for our last night's ghost hunt. Prior to our investigation, a few team members relaxed in the sitting room enjoying the warmth of the fireplace. From another part of the castle, Frank Polievka walked in and began taking digital photos of the lounge's surroundings. After reviewing his photos, one recent picture he shared with the team revealed a menacing ghostly figure seen over the left shoulder of Michael Richards, who was sitting on a sofa. This translucent "head" appeared to be covered with a veil and it could clearly be seen staring directly at Gavin sitting across from it, as Gavin was eerily staring back at it. We all concluded that this anomaly was not caused by a lens flare as Frank's auto flash was off during this series of photos.

Michael is on the left. Gavin on the right sitting with his clenched fists.
Photo by Frank Polievka © 2006

The events of our last night's ghost hunt at Ross Castle were just starting. Prior to climbing the wooden spiral staircase to the third level, Al shared a story of a historical incident that involved a French woman named Alysse, who died in a tragic accident in the same tower we were going to investigate. We decided to try to record some EVPs in hopes of contacting Alysse. I approached Al and asked if it would be reasonable to conduct the EVP session in her native French language. He paused for a few seconds and said that it would make sense to do so. Since I am semi-fluent in French, the task was immediately assigned to me. *Merci beaucoup*...I think.

Our group climbed the steps and settled in a large bedroom on the third floor. After setting up our ghost detecting equipment, we sat in the dark not knowing what to expect. After about forty minutes of hearing diminutive noises that could easily have been anything, suddenly a bright burst of energy appeared near the east wall and quickly vanished after a split second. We were all stunned!

After speaking with each person later in the evening, I learned that they all described the same event. More than one member defined it as an undulating luminosity without a recognizable form. Trying to come up with a rational explanation, we discussed the possibility of a car's headlights shining through one of the 4-inch arrowslits in the bedroom. However, this hypothesis was shot down because the castle was located about a half-mile from any heavily driven roads. Also, having a distant vehicle's dimmed headlight beams through the narrow vertical aperture of the third-story slit also did not make sense. The EVP recordings from our investigation did not reveal any spectral replies.

After packing my belongings and moving on to our next destination, I had the opportunity to chat with the gentleman innkeeper in the kitchen. I shared with him my sense of excitement and awe of my journey in Ireland so far. I told him that I really connected with the rich culture, the rolling hills and pastures, and the traditional music with fiddles and accordions that reminded me of my Québécois childhood upbringing.

I even mentioned that some of the food, such as the black pudding sausage, was akin to our French-Canadian boudin noir. Before we parted ways, we shook hands as I thanked him for our spectacular stay.

Sunday, November 12, 2006
Leap Castle, County Offaly

DCMAG was the first American paranormal group to conduct an official investigation of Leap Castle back in 2004. The castle was originally a fortress built around 1250 CE by the O'Bannon clan. Because of its turbulent history of bloodshed and brutal atrocities, this castle is reputed to be one of the most haunted locations in all of Ireland. According to various internet sources, there have been hundreds of accounts of visitors experiencing fascinating and horrific spirits at Leap Castle, which is one of the reasons that DCMAG decided to investigate this castle…yet, another time.

Following the death of Mulrooney O'Carroll in 1532 many skirmishes within the O'Carroll leadership took place for years. This fighting came to a head one day when one rival brother burst into the castle's chapel and stabbed his brother (who was a priest) while he was holding mass. As a result of the priest's murder, the sanctuary has become known as the Bloody Chapel. Nearly five hundred years later the Bloody Chapel is reportedly one of the most active places in Leap Castle.

The priest's murder was the first of many tragedies that took place at the castle. Some believe that his death may have paved the way for other tragedies, which in turn have led to the hauntings that have wreaked havoc on many visitors and guests who have stayed at the over the years.

Leap Castle also has a hidden 'oubliette' or secret dungeon that was discovered behind a wall in the chapel in the 1920s. This recently discovered oubliette consisted of a nearly ten-foot-deep shaft that at one time had wooden spikes embedded on the floor where unwanted kinfolk would be tossed into and impaled. There, they would die of their wounds in complete darkness. When the forgotten prison was discovered, hundreds of bones from dozens of skeletons were found at the bottom of the pit. After their discovery, the castle occupants arranged to have each skeleton removed and I would imagine that they were given a proper burial.

After driving for about an hour from our last destination in fog and rain, we finally drove through the stone-arched wrought-iron gate to the front entrance of Leap Castle. It was after nightfall, although we were originally scheduled to visit Leap Castle earlier in the afternoon for a late-night investigation only.

However, our commute took longer than expected, which was fine because arriving at the legendary castle after the dark in a heavy fog only added to the shadowy atmosphere of our visit. Barry exited the van and walked over to the ancient wooden door to announce our arrival. He knocked, but there was no answer. He knocked another time, but still the same as the door remained closed. Apparently, our host Sean was not available to slide the latches aside to receive us since we missed our scheduled appointment time. However, we stayed to explore and photograph the primeval castle's exterior structures and hidden openings. Nothing unusual was captured on film except for multiple orbs that were the result of camera flashes reflecting off the light drizzle from the misty weather. Reluctantly, we got back into the van and went on our way toward our next destination, Markree Castle.

Markree Castle, County Sligo
Monday, November 13, 2006

Our final destination was located in Collooney, a town in County Sligo, which was located in the northwestern region of Ireland. Markree Castle is a beautiful gothic castle built in the 1300s on magnificent 500 acres of land. The great poet and playwright W.B. Yeats visited and stayed at Markree castle on many occasions. The estate has endured several battles from opposing clans and a direct invasion from the English and many other turbulent political clashes over the past seven centuries, but the prominent structure has remained intact since its last restoration in the early 1800s.

Barry's passenger van drove under a beautiful stone arch and onto a long, stately driveway that led to the front entrance of Markree Castle. Fortunately, Barry had our rooms reserved in advance so we straightforwardly walked past a grand fireplace inside the main foyer, climbed the regal oak staircase, then I passed under a majestic stained glass window that led us down a long hallway and into our individual bedrooms.

According to Al, legend has it that there is a resident ghost that occupies the estate and Room 7 was supposedly the area where the activity was most active. However, Frank and Jonathan shared this room undisturbed by paranormal happenings for a couple of nights. After an afternoon of self-guided exploration of Markree Castle, we met in the grand dining room for dinner. From a menu of entrees that were pre-selected earlier, I had an appetizer of smoked chicken fillet with roasted almonds & exotic dressing and the main course of sirloin steak medallions cooked in whiskey pepper sauce with a side of tender-crisp green beans, with a glass of Emiliana Cabernet Sauvignon.

Early the next morning, we hopped back into the 'Mystery Machine' and drove to the town of Sligo to buy gifts for loved ones back in the States. Afterward, we were driven to the picturesque Garavogue River and took a short stroll to the Fiddler's Creek Bar for a late lunch. We found a few empty tables next to round slatestone columns and ordered drinks. I decided to experience an authentic pint of the world-famous Guinness beer. Before long, we received our glugs and as I watched my dark and creamy stout settle down like a midnight fog, I asked Barry who was sitting at the other side of the table a question, "Baz, what are you drinking there?" He replied, "This is a Budweiser!" With a smile, I raised my 'pint of gat' and said, "Naturally." My meal soon arrived on a huge plate, which was covered with thick slices of roasted turkey breast with gravy, stuffing with mixed herbs, with a side of creamy colcannon, and a warm loaf of brown bread. Cheers!

When the group returned to Markree Castle for the evening, we gathered into the grand lodge that had been decked with Victorian furniture for a nightcap. There, we sat under a large bay window with a grand view of the estate's backyard. I was still energized from the day's outing and was wanting to delve into this castle further prior to ordering my drink. I snuck away and took a walk down the grand hall and noticed a half-opened door next to a barista station. As I peeked through this opening, I saw stairs going into the basement. Naturally, being the person I am, I thought, "Ooh, yeah!"

166

The dimmed stairwell light was on, so I descended into this ancient cellar.

Once on the bottom, I saw the ceiling had large concrete-like arches as main supports, most of which had some longstanding lime-based plaster that was flaking away. A pile of lumber and other construction material was arranged neatly along one wall while an old dusty piano stood at the other end of this room. A third wall had a doorway, so naturally, I went through it. This area had a few rooms with multiple storage shelves and just around the corner, I found another area that held many ale kegs with beverage tubing feeding upward through the floor above me. I concluded that I was directly beneath the lounge's bar. There were other wooden doors that led to additional chambers within this ancient labyrinth, but after hearing a few clamors echoing from behind them, I realized that it was time for me to quickly return to the lads above to quench my thirst. Unnoticed, I quietly walked in and ordered myself a Smithwick's Irish red ale for the first time, which was exceptional.

The Curse of the Lisheen House, Sligo
Tuesday, November 14, 2006

Our last day's expedition first led us to the northwestern tip of Ireland to explore the cliff-lined Mullaghmore Coast that overlooks the North Atlantic Ocean. We also made a quick stop-over in Drumcliffe Parish Church Cemetery to visit the gravestone of famous Irish poet W. B. Yeats' set against the grandiose backdrop of the colossal flat-topped rock of Benbulgen Mountain.

Barry Fitzgerald on the left. Photo by Frank Polievka © 2006

DCMAG team and I were in for a rare treat for our last afternoon in Ireland. After being given permission from the property owner, we were allowed to visit the Lisheen House, which is described as one of the most daunting ruins near the coastal town of Strandhill. It was a large, abandoned stone and brick manor without a roof, almost totally concealed behind trees and shrubbery. Prior to entering the field near the manor, Barry conveyed to the group two important rules that had to be respected:

Rule #1: Do not collect any broken artifacts within this structure as shards, metal fragments, debris, and so forth.

Rule #2: Please stay away from the 'fairy-rath' or ringforts that are in the nearby sacred ground. (The ringforts are ancient circular mounds that Irish folklore describes as being built by fairies or the little people.)

Depending on who you ask, the history of the Lisheen House will vary quite a bit. However, I will do my best to share the basics. The mansion was built by William Phibbs in the late 1700s. His son Owen was a reputed archaeologist who collected artifacts from the Far East, Egypt, and Syria and displayed them on the first floor. Rumor had Owen Phibbs' private collection of artifacts even included a mummy brought back from one of his expeditions from Egypt.

According to many internet accounts, strange incidents began to be reported throughout the house after Owen Phibbs brought the mummy to his home. For a long time, strange sounds and loud crashes could be heard throughout the night from unknown sources. When Phibbs investigated, he found that many of the ancient relics and pottery he acquired had inexplicably shattered on the floor. One of the domestic servants also reportedly witnessed a tall shadowy figure wander the property. Shortly after,

Phibbs refused to stay at the Lisheen House and they all departed. The house remained vacant until Jesuits priests were called in to get rid of the spirits that had taken over the house. Unfortunately, the priests were unable to eradicate the house of this ethereal infestation.

After unsuccessfully trying to clear his home of the paranormal activity, the disenchanted owner sold the property in the mid-1930s and cleared out all of its contents. Nobody moved back into the house and it eventually became abandoned and exposed to the elements. What remains of the house today is just a ghostly façade overgrown with thick ivy vines and trees growing throughout; a force of nature reclaiming the land.

The abandoned Lisheen House.   Norman Gagnon © 2006

Exploration:

Once we agreed to the rules, the team split up and we examined inside of this archaic, crumbling structure along with its outer yard. Deteriorating plaster debris was scattered about the dirt floor mixed with dried leaves and broken branches from the canopy of trees branches above. Astonishingly, in some areas, the thick vines growing throughout the building appeared to be the only support holding up the brick walls. In other areas, the building appeared like a house of cards barely held together by a few internal doorway frames.

The fireplace on the first floor had black soot fused within the inner walls of the chimney. I looked up to the roofless top and saw another fireplace fascia eerily suspended above. The remnants of the ceiling joists that separated the first and second floor jutted out and could barely be seen in the shadows.

The house outside the perimeter had a few small arched glassless windows half-hidden behind tall grass. These openings led into darkened underground chambers. One of these basement transoms was obstructed by two small trees, as the thought of the Celtic goddess Danu came to mind as if she dared anybody to cross this barrier. Although it was abandoned, this place was astonishingly beautiful. However, after a while, I had to step outside and walk a few yards from the house to take a break from the exploration.

Although I did not experience anything out of the ordinary at the Lisheen House, the return trip to Markree Castle was another story. While driving back, Barry became unusually bewildered and we got lost. This was not really characteristic of Barry, who generally knows his way around this amazing island. In any case, we returned to Markree Castle much later than we had expected. I can only wonder if the visit to the manor had anything to do with Barry's disorientation.

Back at the Markree castle, we regrouped and exchanged field notes from our assessment of the abandoned site. Later that evening, we discovered that someone in our group broke both the rules we had been warned about. This individual walked over one of the ringforts to look around and had also picked up related 'mementos' from the Lisheen ruins and other places we explored. When Barry found out, he was not a jovial lad that evening. The malevolent objects were soon discarded...followed by a slap on the wrist. I'm not quite sure why a few members of the team started to behave rather unfavorably at the tail end of our expedition. Perhaps being exposed to numerous haunted sites that were infused with malicious pasts, or simply enduring symptoms of the jet lag disorder.

On November 14, 2006, we got up at 4:00 a.m. and groggily packed our bags, and were driven to Dublin International Airport, as it was a very long and quiet ride. The flight back across the pond went well though.

About eight months after our expedition to Ireland, the TAPS' Ghost Hunters with Pilgrim Studios production team visited the Lisheen House and Leap Castle along with other haunted sites for a two-episode special for SyFy's '*Ghost Hunters*' series in 2007. The TAPS team was also guided by my friend Barry, who eventually became the co-host for the spinoff series '*Ghost Hunters International*' (GHI) from 2008 to 2012!

As a final note, I would like to thank our paranormal host Barry 'Baz" Fitzgerald for his hospitality and patience in guiding us through the beautiful Emerald Isle and revealing to us a few of its mysterious secrets!

Chapter Six: Risk of Contacting Spirits

"The instant, however, that I had stepped over the threshold, he moved impulsively forward, and holding out his hand grasped mine with a strength which made me wince"
- Bram Stoker's Dracula, 1897

I have often cautioned fellow paranormal investigators about making attempts to contact the 'other side' by means such as Ouija boards, séances, spirit boxes, or other interrelated instruments because doing so can be unsafe in my view. I am not implying that these objects have supernatural conductivities to unlock and communicate with unknown realms but rather, having a living soul that is willing to take the first step to open themselves to interconnect with these forces.

I personally do not conduct electronic voice phenomena sessions anymore; once bitten, twice shy. I will explain my reasons in more detail later in this chapter. That being said, I still utilize digital recorders, video cameras, and sensors in my field investigations to record any paranormal incidents that may take place. In my experience, if a ghost wants to talk or throw a perilous tantrum, it can do so without being prompted or provoked. I believe the act of interacting with these entities would be the equivalent of taking part in an ethereal Russian roulette; the spinning cylinder will at some point align with the firing chamber, which will then propel a malevolent force into your life.

Stepping over this threshold, whether it be by contacting the spirit world, sauntering through 'high risk' areas such as midnight jaunts through a graveyard, or taking part in risky rituals or occult practices, may lure unwanted shadows into your life. I have personally witnessed a case where an investigator has been the unwilling target of such malevolence.

On September 14, 2007, I joined Maryland's newly established AdventureMyths paranormal investigative team led by fellow investigator Frank Polievka. We teamed up to conduct the investigation at the South Mountain Civil War Battlefield in Middletown, Maryland, on the eve of the 145th anniversary of the Battle of South Mountain that took placed in 1862. After setting up camp near the Appalachian Trail, we discovered an old stone wall inside a dense forest within the battlefield. At sundown, I accompanied Frank, Jonathan Ness, Michael Richards, and a Civil War enthusiast to an isolated area on the battlefield to conduct an EVP session. Strangely enough shortly after we started, the woods developed an unexpected fog. While a couple of team members asked EVP questions, I took digital photos of the darkened surroundings. The last photo I captured was of a 'burst of energy' that covered the face of the team's sensitive Michael Richards.

Michael was sitting about ten feet from me and to my left when I captured this photo below.

Michael on the left with his face obstructed by an energy burst. Frank with the hat in the center.   Photo by Norman Gagnon © 2007

Just as I was about to notify what I just captured on camera, we all heard a moan come from Michael. We immediately went to him to see if he was alright. He told us that he had suddenly become very disoriented and nauseated. After a few minutes, he felt well enough to walk back to our camp. After we settled down to have a late dinner, I reviewed this one digital photo again and shared it with the team. I then concluded that I may have essentially photographed the precise moment when this entity made "contact" with Michael!

176

This AdventureMyths video from our investigation (including the "contact" photograph) can be viewed at this YouTube link: https://www.youtube.com/watch?v=zww5s1M_-_Q

A little more about Michael Richards. I first met Michael at my first DC Metro Area Ghost Watchers (DCMAG) meeting in Alexandria, Virginia, in 2003. Al Tyas, DCMAG's founder and chief, introduced him as the team's "sensitive", as he was able to sense and often see these manifestations within his environment that were undetectable to the rest of us. The way I perceive this ability, it is perhaps like a radio transceiver that can both transmit and receive communications. In Michael's case, his body may also emit a frequency that can only be perceived within the spiritual realm's perspective. Therefore, as we began or "switched on" the EVP transmission, it may have attracted a curious entity that immediately drifted towards Michael's 'aura' to make contact. The result of this unsafe interaction could have been much worse. Later that evening, he took me aside and said, "Norm, we should have not contacted these spirits. As you may be aware that the Bible forbids this type of activity."

Here's an example of what Michael is referring to that I would like to share. This is one of several passages from this ancient tome on the subject of communicating with the dead:

'There must not be found among you anyone who makes his son or daughter pass through the fire, or uses secret ways, or does witchcraft, or tells the meaning of special things, or is a witch, [11] or uses secret power on people, or helps people talk to spirits, or talks to spirits himself, or talks with the dead.' (Deuteronomy 18:10-11).

Michael's experience at the South Mountain Civil War Battlefield was very unnerving. However, it was by no means unique. Over the years I have received many emails through my SEARCH account, several of which were from parents of young teenagers who have had strange experiences soon after they attempted to dabble with communing with spirits. These incidents varied slightly from case to case, but usually dark shadows are seen, doors slamming shut, dishes falling off the shelf and smashing onto the floors, and in one incident involving a family dog that was staring and growling at an empty corner of the living room for over fifteen minutes.

One of the first questions I always ask on my visits is whether they or their kids have taken part in an Ouija board gathering in the past. Often, their reply would be something along the lines of, "Yes, but just once at a sleepover." This sounds innocent enough but this anonymous quote reveals, "When you invite trouble, it is usually quick to accept."

I am certain that some of you are asking this question. "Norm, if you are so concerned about not communicating with spirits of the dead, why do you investigate haunted places?" Well, ask yourself this. When the fire department is called in for a house fire, are the firefighters' purpose is to bask themselves in the warm glow of the flames – or to put out the fire before it can spread?

When I am asked to investigate a potentially haunted house, my purpose is to assist the family on how to get rid of their troublesome drifter. This eviction will of course have to be agreed upon with all of the household members. First, I would suggest that they discard the object(s) used to make contact with the spirit realm. Next, I ask about their religious *affiliation*, denomination, or belief system, and then request if they be willing to invite a spiritual leader into their home for a blessing, prayer, or cleansing ceremony and the like, to expel this specter out of their home before it escalates into something much more aggressive.

Ghostly Manifestations

The following segment is about a young man named Den who emailed me to disclose the many abnormal and often terrifying incidents that he witnessed as a young boy and continued into his adulthood. He admitted that he visited a few places that he shouldn't have been due to his curiosity. I tried asking him about what took place in his early life that might have incited these manifestations.

However, he did not want to divulge any of the details of his youth.

Was he persuaded to take part in a ceremony of sorts that exposed himself to these demonic harassments? Although he was hesitant to tell me anything at first, Dan eventually did start to trust me more. Here are some of the strange encounters he was willing to share with me.

In October 2005 I received my first email from Den, who at the time was a Lance Corporal in the United States Marine Corps. The subject line from Den's first email was '*Weird Happenings in my Hometown*'. This definitely caught my attention. After doing some research, I learned that the hometown that Den referred to was Granby, Connecticut.

Town's History

Granby was founded in 1723 when a group of residents from nearby Simsbury decided to form their own community. Granby became officially known as an independent settlement by 1786. Nearly thirty years prior to the infamous Salem Witch Trials, Granby had its own series of witch persecutions that took place from 1647 to 1697 that resulted in a total of eleven people being hanged for witchcraft.

In addition to the witch trials, Granby was well-known for

the New Gate Prison, which is known hot spot for paranormal encounters. The site of the prison stands on acreage that was first used as a colonial-era copper mine from 1707 to 1745. The mine was fashioned by tunneling a large vertical shaft, which in turn branched out into multiple horizontal passageways dug at different levels. In 1773 New-Gate Prison was built on the site of one of the empty copper mines. Rather than build cells for the prisoners, they were housed in the abandoned mine shafts with little protection from the elements and very little ventilation. Prisoners lived underground from 1773 until New-Gate Prison closed in 1827. When this underground prison closed, all of the remaining prisoners were transferred to the newly built Wethersfield State Prison.

Between Granby's own history of witch trials and New-Gate Prison, I could easily see why there could be weird happenings taking place in Den's hometown. Over the next several weeks, Den sent me a number of emails detailing some of these paranormal experiences from when he was a teenager. In one email, Den revealed that he tried to 'connect' to the other side. However, he did not provide any details about how he had attempted to do so. Here is an excerpt from Den's first email to me.

"Well, to begin with my town is rumored to have had Satanic and witchcraft-based goings-on for the past 200 years. I myself have come across some very strange and frightening things. You've gotta understand I'm not easily scared. I'm currently in the Marine Corps so you know that I'm not easily shaken."

Further emails described when he was in his mid-teens, Den and his friend decided to go into the woods located behind his friend's house to light firecrackers just before sundown. After a while of lighting firecrackers and filling the area with smoke, Den and his friend noticed a bright light had appeared behind them. Thinking they must have attracted the attention of a neighboring homeowner, they took off running down a trail and hid among the trees. Den saw that the light was moving closer through the trees at a rapid pace but noticed there was no sound of footsteps or of anybody shouting at them. A short time later, Den and his friend ran out of the forest into an open field and up a hill that overlooked Manitook Lake.

As they stopped to catch their breath, Den looked back and saw that the light appeared to be floating several feet above the ground to the same elevation they were. They estimated that the hill was approximately seventy feet above the field. Den and his friend backtracked toward their home, but the light still pursued them. Looking at the light, Den estimated that it must have been about eight feet off the ground. When they ran out of the forest and into the field behind his friend's house, the light stopped at the edge of the woods and disappeared. Den added in his email,

"I know I was not hallucinating or anything but it really freaked me the hell out…that I cannot explain by myself and nobody believed me."

In another email, Den explained that shortly after he came home from boot camp in 2004, he and a friend were riding their ATVs in some nearby fields just before sunset. As Den and his friend approached a clearing that they were both familiar with, Den's ATV struck a hidden depression in the ground. Den jumped off and realized that he had badly cut his hand. Before administering first-aid, he inspected the ATV and was relieved to find that it had not been damaged in the accident. However, Den and his friend noticed an old hidden tombstone a few feet from where he crashed the ATV.

After taking care of his hand, Den and his friend decided to return home. Almost immediately, they heard rustling coming from the forest just a few yards away. They aimed their flashlight beams toward the sound to find out what kind of animal was causing it. Den wrote he was shocked by what he saw, "What we saw next totally freaked me the hell out. It looked to be perhaps a girl in raggedy clothes and long gangly hair. She was just slowly walking through the woods. We tore the hell outta there!"

For the next three months that followed, Den continued to correspond with me disclosing more paranormal encounters that he experienced while in the town of Granby. He said that over the years he began to believe that he seems to attract these types of frightening incidents. He shared that he felt like there is an evil force that wanted to harm him.

For fun or simple curiosity, did Den unwillingly open a door that summoned a dark force into his life?

Vaporous Mist on Photographs

I have seen many photographs on web pages from ghost chasing enthusiasts depicting smoke-like streaks in their shots. Of course, some of these film anomalies were caused by the camera flash illuminating strands of long hair, smoke from a nearby campfire, lit cigarettes, or simply light reflecting off the fog's condensed water vapors. But I have noticed these opaque streaks on photos that are very strange, many of which were captured during daylight conditions without the use of a flash.

I had a friend who had a history of panic attacks. Over the years, I learned to tell when he was suffering from one. If he had a panic attack and could not leave his home, we would simply stay at his place, order a pizza, and watch a movie.

After his death in 2015, I looked through a shoebox of photographs that he took over the years. I noticed that in several photos there were strange 'vaporous bands' that seemed to encircle my friend's face or within his lens' range. One specific photograph had several horizontal bands swirling throughout the photo, as it reminded me of a Hollywood movie of storm-chasers being trapped into the eye of a perilous tornado, frightfully observing streaks of smoke and dust from pulverized debris encircling them.

As for the photographs from my friend's collection, it is unlikely that the vapor trails in these photos were caused by the camera malfunction. If it had been an isolated case, I would have believed that. However, I have seen several other internet photographs taken by ghost hunters with similar unexplained streaks. When I ask them for their opinions, I generally get the usual answer as they would call these 'ghostly spirits'.

I have my own opinions as to what some of these vapor trails captured in photographs actually are. What if they are manifestations that are actually encircling the photographer? I noticed that sometimes during an investigation, a fellow ghost hunter may feel a sudden sensation of a surge of cold air or even feel disoriented. It is almost as if they are experiencing an immediate "panic attack" seconds after the entity brushes against them. When I looked at these photos later, I would often see the familiar vaporous streaks. Is there a connection?

I have a simple hypothesis. Are some of these panic attacks the direct result of the investigator or photographer being in contact with the source of these vaporous anomalies? I have wondered if there may be some form of intelligence behind them. Unlike anxiety attacks caused by some underlying stressor or threat, can a person who has had no history of panic attacks unexpectedly experience one on a paranormal outing, as these may be considered as high-risk environments for such supernatural clashes?

For a few weeks or so in 2008, I have personally experienced my first series of *panic attacks*. Here's my account. First, let me say that I am relatively healthy, I was not nor am I now taking medication of any sort, and I am a non-smoker. When I experienced my first "attack", I was attending a Mutual UFO Network meeting at a local bar & grill restaurant. The attendees at these meetings vary from field investigators, ghost hunters, paranormal researchers, and a few peculiars that usually sit quietly in the back of the room. All of the sudden during my meal, I felt my heart stop beating for just a few seconds. Just as I was about to blackout, my heart kicked in high gear as it kept me from passing out head-first into my salad. These irregular heart palpitation sessions occurred in three rapid waves within a minute's time until the symptoms suddenly stopped. Sitting in a cold sweat, I began to…well panic a little, which was not helping my situation at all.

So, I sat there, took a few deep breaths, and tried to remain calm. Upon my drive back home, I understood then what these unfortunate people experience during their anxiety outbreaks. Supernaturally speaking, was this some sort of assault projected onto me by someone in the meeting or perhaps a wraith that may have affixed themselves to me from one of my field investigations?

The irregular heart palpitations would come and go randomly for a few weeks. Interestingly enough, I noticed that the symptoms got much, much worse during a church service, as I also broke out into cold sweats. Remarkably enough, this started to make sense to me. This was a sign that it was time to embark in a *spiritual decompression chamber* if you will. With meditation, prayer and pretty much turning up the volume of my Christian faith, the panic attacks did cease. This was a well-needed cleansing, my friends!

In any case, back to the vapor streaks in my departed friend's stack of photos. He was not a smoker, and at the time the outdoor photos were taken, it was too warm for these misty clouds to be generated by his breath due to cold weather. I never really had the chance to gently ask him if he or a family member had any interests in the paranormal, but needless to say he is now resting in peace.

Here's a supposition for all paranormal investigators to consider. If you seem to be capturing these ghostly manifestations on film (vapors, streaks, vortexes, etc.), it may be an indicator that these anomalies may be orbiting around you.

Cover of Darkness

"It is best to avoid the beginnings of evil"

– Henry David Thoreau

For years I have correlated many high-strangeness cases specifically to intrusive entities that breach through their dimension and into our world. These manifestations often take place in bedrooms and often in the middle of the night when the sleeping targets are most vulnerable. There have been many reports about people being attacked by supernatural entities for thousands of years throughout the world. In the past, they were referred to as the night hag, incubus, maron-demon (Old Germanic for *nightmare*), and so forth. More recently, the bedroom infiltrations are entities that are now described as anything from shadow people to alien humanoids. Do these creatures have the capability to metamorphize themselves to any form they chose to suit their hidden purposes? Perhaps we are focusing too much on their outer appearance rather than their true intent.

Here is an example of what a witness would likely report during an interview that may lead credence to my hypothesis: "I suddenly woke up and I couldn't move my body, as if I was paralyzed, then I saw a [FILL IN THE BLANK] at the foot of my bed!" This is a common account given by many who have experienced these hellish intrusions.

Another observation I would like to make is that in most cases, these entities seem to have the ability to control people cognitively and physically. Victims often report that they feel frozen in bed and many also feel intense pressure on their chests. These entities also appear to have the capability of communicating with their victims telepathically. After the terrifying experience, the being would frequently levitate off the floor to exit the bedroom by phasing through a wall or ceiling, leaving behind some confused and mentally shaken soul.

What exactly are these entities? Dare we give them such labels as aliens, demons, ghosts, or shadow people? I believe that the answer may depend on your core belief system, your personal philosophy, or your religious background. In my view, these creatures can manifest themselves as a form that may be based on our own worldview or cultural background.

These types of home invasions have repeatedly taken place throughout our history.

There are several works of art and written testimonies that depict beasts in women sleeping chambers. The 1781 painting *'Nightmare'* by Swiss artist Henry Fuseli captures the fear associated with such encounters. It depicts an incubus sitting on top of the tormented woman trapped in her bed. Please note the diabolic horse in this portrait, as this may represent a symbol of the *vessel* that transported this beast into her chamber.

Oil on canvas by Henry Fuseli 1781. Detroit Institute of Arts

People that are not familiar with paranormal investigation may ask if there are any malicious intentions behind these nighttime incursions. Well, let's see. They trespass. They cause paralysis. They violate our homes, thoughts, and well-being, all under cover of darkness.

So, I would say that yes, there is definitely malicious intent. In this chapter, I just skimmed the surface of the potential risks in experimenting with the "other side". I have a question for the researchers or thrill-seekers who try to communicate with these spirits. Do you honestly believe that you will receive an honest and truthful answer-back? Take another look at the beast sitting on top of the woman's torso.

I can see the appeal of joining a group of ghost hunters and going into an old, abandoned structure hoping to capture ghostly apparitions on film for your scrapbook or website gallery. What is your real intent? Are you seeking thrill and chills, or perhaps to prove life after death exists, or is the purpose of your investigations is to help tormented living souls who are asking for help and elucidation of what is really going?

Chapter Seven: The Orb Phenomenon

There are many plausible hypotheses that could explain the aerial illuminations that have been witnessed by countless people for thousands of years across the globe. Depending on the specific point in history and cultural reference, these drifting lights have been referred to as will-o'-wisps, ghost lights, foo fighters, orbs, and so forth.

This chapter will not cover earth lights, ball lightning, or manmade objects as sky lanterns and military flares. Rather, I will focus on these mysterious luminescent objects that seem to have an intelligence all their own. So, what are they really?

Imagine if you will this scenario. A ghost hunter walks into a graveyard late at night for an investigation and comes face-to-face with a brilliant glowing orb hovering over an old mausoleum. Before the ghost hunter can process what is occurring, the orb swiftly flies into the air about 100 feet. Luckily, he managed to capture a digital photo before it disappeared behind a thick canopy of trees. To everybody who would listen, the ghost hunter would proclaim, "I saw a spirit-light and I have proof!"

Unknown to the ghost hunter about half a block away a group of ufologists is conducting an unrelated investigation then they unexpectedly see the same orb drifting above an abandoned warehouse before it whooshes away at a 45-degree angle into the darkness of space above. The team leader was fortunate enough to film his encounter. He tells his team, "This was definitely a UFO and we caught it on video!"

I myself have seen these bright lights on two occasions, as they hovered at a distance for less than a minute, often pulsating until they simply blinked out and disappear. So, I believe it is sensible to not necessarily jump to conclusions about what they are or where they came from. However, we can all agree that these manifestations are, or derive from, an intelligent source.

I have had the opportunity to interview several people who have had experiences with these bright objects. As most of these unidentified anomalies appear to be some sort of energy and in one case, it was indeed glowing from within but its radiant source appeared to be contained inside a translucent spherical "shell" as to those plasma ball lamps sold at novelty shops. Thus, I would like to disclose eight reports that are from my MUFON files archive that I categorized under the orb phenomenon for this chapter. In most of my witness testimonies, the orbs were observed from a safe distance but there were a couple incidents that these glowing spheres have drifted a little too close to the eyewitnesses.

MUFON Case: 41609

Location: Union Hall, Virginia

Date of Event: August 9, 2012

Date of Assignment: August 10, 2012

Investigator: Norman Gagnon

Witnesses reported that on August 9, 2012, at approximately 10:45 p.m., they all observed a series of orange lights/orbs over a lake in Union Hall, Virginia.

Three boys were on a dock located on the southwestern shores of Smith Mountain Lake enjoying the warm evening breeze. They all found their attention suddenly drawn to a series of strange lights that were slowly hovering above the lake. The young men ran to the cabin to announce to everyone about the strange lights they have just seen. One of the young men's mothers, "SM", her sister, and her father all scurried out to the dock to observe a string of ten orange lights ascending upward into the night sky and disappearing into the clouds.

The orbs were spaced apart and only two were visible whooshing upwards at a time, systemically taking turns. The sighting lasted approximately 10 minutes and the orange lights did not generate any sound nor any propulsion sources were evident as they continuously remained lit (no blinking or strobing).

SM described the experience to me during an interview. "As two disappeared at its highest point (into the clouds), another pair would come up slightly above the lake's surface. Meanwhile, that would leave a duo at the halfway point. Two lights were the most we saw at a time but there were a total of ten over the 10 minutes. These vessels all followed the exact same path and seemed to be quite evenly spaced".

I asked SM why she used the term "vessels" to describe these lights in her incident report. She replied, "I'm not sure why I used that term...just assumed they were powered and were being piloted".

MUFON CAG International Case: 48790
Location: Ontario, Canada
Date of Event: July 3, 2013
Date of Assignment: July 7, 2013
Investigator: Norman Gagnon

The eyewitness, who I will refer to as 'HC', is a 43-year old woman who claimed to have had a UFO encounter on July 3, 2013, at her residence. HC stated that at approximately 10:10 p.m., she was on her patio when she looked up and saw a bright glowing sphere of light with a tail hovering high above her backyard.

HC described the object as an orb that was bright yellow-orange in color. She offered a more detailed description of the anomaly in her MUFON Case Management System (CMS) report. "There also appeared to be a marbling effect continuously changing within the object which appeared to be swirling in a light of orange, yellow, and white as though it was a chemical or gas not properly mixing."

She estimated that it was about two feet (65cm) in diameter and hovered about 25 feet (7m) off the ground near neighbors' rooftops. The small sphere also had a translucent extension in the rear. The way she described it reminded me of a horizontal stabilizer. HC said she could see swirls of energy flowing inside and she added, "The tail also seemed to be in two parts whereby one was a bit shorter than the other, branching off or forking with the one being a bit shorter. Absolutely no sound was heard."

Illustration by Norman Gagnon © 2013

HC added that the sphere was so bright that it lit up the area within its flight path between her neighbors' homes and above her house. "This object flew very closely at the roofline level and was in the area for about a minute or a minute and a half. I feel it was some sort of collection device such as a scout vehicle."

I learned of a second witness who witnessed the same anomaly. HC wrote, "One of my son's friends saw this object from the front only but did not see the tail extension." Her sighting was very short, just a few seconds. It flashed and pulsed three times from how she described it, and it shot off very quickly."

During an investigation, it is a protocol to acquire as many observations as possible to ensure that the report is thoroughly and accurately completed. In this case, the electricity to area homes and streetlights were not affected. There was no discharge of gas, exhaust, or any particles/dust seen being expelled or dropped during the orb's flight. There appeared to be no damage (burning, melting, warping, etc.,) to area home vinyl sidings or foliage from nearby trees that were near to where the glowing orb was seen hovering.

The possibility of a drone or other remote-control device was ruled out because no high-pitched buzzing from propellers was heard. HC also added that her dogs did not react negatively to this object.

MUFON Case: 36293

Location: Above Chase City, Virginia

Date of Event: February 18, 2012

Date of Assignment: March 6, 2012

Investigator: Norman Gagnon

This case has been selected by the MUFON Science Review Board as one of the top ten UFO cases in 2012.

On February 18, 2012, around 2:00 p.m., a father and son (John) pilot-team was flying from Charlotte, North Carolina to Richmond, Virginia in their Mooney Ovation II aircraft. While en route, the plane flew dangerously close to an unidentified glowing anomaly (orb) that seemed to follow directly along their flight path. Following the Federal Aviation Administration's IFR (Instrument Flight Rules), the plane was flying at a speed of 188 knots (approximately 216 miles per hour) at an altitude of 7480 feet when it crossed from North Carolina into Virginia. Later as the plane was preparing to land at the Richmond International Airport, the son searched the sky for air traffic when something caught his attention.

All of the sudden, John saw a large glowing sphere flying close to the plane's right-wing as the object got within about fifty feet from the plane. At that instant, the guidance and electrical equipment suddenly lost power! John added that the plane's engine did not fully shut down; it sputtered a little but as the orb disappeared from view at an incredible rate of speed, the plane's equipment became operational again.

Illustration by Norman Gagnon © 2012

John made the following quote during the interview of the incident. "As far as instruments affected, the altimeter, altitude indicator, magnetic compass, course deviation indicators, and electrical function of the craft were affected. This was all within a few moments as soon as we recognized we were being paralleled by the object. The UFO accelerated away to a speed I can't even calculate out of sight to our 12 o'clock…I've never in my life had seen anything like this happen. It was much unexpected because we did not see the vehicle approach. This vehicle was about thirty feet in diameter, which glowed and may have had a solid shape beneath the energy.

What I could observe on the surface which seemed to have some circular swirling energy force which surrounded something I believed operated it from within." When I asked John if I could interview his father, John told me that his father refused and he just wanted to put this disturbing incident behind him.

After reviewing the case notes and reading the son's testimony, it is my belief that this anomaly may have generated a non-nuclear, high-powered electromagnetic pulse of energy that disrupted the plane's electrical system. An electromagnetic pulse (EMP) has the potential to disrupt unprotected critical instruments and in the case of this small plane, the EMP radiation generated by this unknown object may have caused the plane to temporarily lose its electrical system for a few seconds. Luckily, the orb rapidly flew away and the plane soon regained its flight system to the point where they shortly made a safe landing.

MUFON Case: 39830

Location: Berryville, Virginia

Date of Event: June 25, 2012

Date Submitted: June 26, 2012

Investigator: Norman Gagnon

"PM" a 16-year-old boy reported that on June 25, 2012, he witnessed a large, bright orange object hovering over a nearby housing community about 300 feet from his backyard, a little after midnight. Shortly after, the UAP emitted a bright white beam from below it.

The witnesses (PM) and his younger brother were watching television. A little after midnight, PM noticed a strong light radiating through their living room window, as they both got up and ran to see. The glowing sphere was very large and it just stood there, stationary. Twelve minutes later, it emitted a white beam for about two minutes and he believed the beam may have ended at the ground level but his view was obstructed by backyard bushes. Shortly after, the UAP blinked out and disappeared at 12:20 a.m.

PM described this incident to me during our interview. "The bright light was so large that it lit my backyard and the houses below it. It did not make any noise but the trees right below it did move and sway but there was really no heavy wind that night…this bright light at first made me feel terrified of it but a few minutes later, I just felt as if as it was supposed to be there."

MUFON Case: 82365

Location: Stafford, Virginia

Date of Event: February 25, 2017

Date of Assignment: February 26, 2017

Investigator: Norman Gagnon

On February 25, 2017, at approx. 08:30 PM, the witness "JD" from the back deck of his home, located in Stafford, Virginia, observed a bright light silently hovering nearby for about 40 minutes. A photo was submitted.

JD: "This photograph was taken using a cellular camera Saturday in Stafford Virginia on 25 Feb 17 around 9:35pm behind my house. I noticed a bright white light object hovering above the school parking lot over scattered homes and a wooded area lot, about 200 to 500 feet above the tree line. The object appeared about 1,250 yards away. I stood on the deck and took the picture, the light was silent and made no sound, it was there longer than 40 minutes, I thought maybe it was a helicopter or plane coming toward me, giving the illusion of a stationary light, but it just stayed hovering for a long time, no change is size or dimension.

My wife also witnessed that object with me and she thinks she may have seen it again later that night but it slightly moved to the right."

Investigator's note: The photo shows the anomaly being a bright, white light only, but if it had any other colors as red or green and as it was flown from a school's parking lot, it could have been a drone however the battery life for these commercial drones are 15 to 20 minutes long (sighting was over 40 minutes).

EXIF image data results: Photo taken with a Samsung SM N910A at 08:37 p.m. February 25, 2017. Auto exposure, Program AE, 1/8sec., f/2.2, ISO 1000.

JD's background: In his mid-50s, NAVY-US Military Senior Intelligence Analyst with a security clearance of TS/SCI and CI Polygraph.

MUFON Case: 43254

Location: over Richmond, Virginia

Date of Event: October 14, 2012

Date Submitted: October 14, 2012

Investigator: Norman Gagnon

Illustration by Norman Gagnon © 2012

On October 14, 2012, approx. 07:00 p.m., a jetliner was
about 10 minutes from landing in Richmond International Airport
from Atlanta's Hartsfield-Jackson Airport. A passenger who I will
refer to as 'SN' looked out her window and noticed eight bright
lights drifting in a serpentine pattern above a few buildings below.
Less than a minute later, the lights shot straight up at an incredible
speed and disappeared into the evening sky. She saw that several
other passengers noticed the lights, who began to murmur in
excitement. SN also stated that these lights left behind some sort
of residue that appeared to be dusty and smoke-like, similar to a jet
trail.

During the interview, SN went into more detail about her experience. "I did also hear the other passengers react with awe by the spectacle of these mysterious lights!"

SN described more of her experience in detail. "We were about 10-12 minutes away from landing, and I noticed a strange series of five to eight bright yellow-orange lights in a horizontal line that was hovering above some buildings in the city below. They suddenly formed into a circle and then continued to form in a straight vertical line. All at once, they shot straight up into the sky, leaving behind a vapor trail. If I heard others correctly on my side of the plane (left side, same as me), they were asking, 'What was that...did you see that?' So, I'm pretty sure that I was not the only one. I felt nervous, especially since I was on an airplane that was already turbulent. I tried to think of military tests, fireworks, airshows, etc., but I haven't been able to form a reasonable conclusion to what I saw tonight on the airplane."

MUFON Case: 57798

Location: Narrows, Virginia

Date of Event: July 4, 2014

Date Submitted: July 7, 2014

Investigator: Norman Gagnon

Witness saw an orange-colored "orb" slowly approaching his location while waiting for the fireworks display to begin.

On July 4th at 9:15 p.m. the witness "BR" noticed an orange light slowly fly slowly toward his location. The object was brightly illuminated that he believed that everyone could clearly see it. When I interviewed him, BR assured me that he knew what he saw. BR, "This craft was clearly NOT a Chinese lantern, a weather balloon, the planet Venus or the other "usual suspects" trotted out after such an event." The sighting lasted for about four minutes then reversing direction hovering back towards a southerly trajectory, then it just blinks out, disappearing from sight.

After he confirmed that the light was not mundane, BR continued with answering my questions. "As far as the craft's direction or position from my vantage point, I'd again be relegated to approximating, but upon referencing Google Maps, and zooming in to find the directional alignment /azimuth associated with Rowland Street,

I'd estimate the craft to have been positioned in the general direction of Dublin, Virginia, (10 miles away) and slightly southeast of the town, but at a distance of at least several miles away."

When I interview an eyewitness, I always ask about his or her profession. When I asked BR about his occupation he replied: "Although I'll balk at a direct response to this question, I will say, however, that I'm not a professional pilot, nor affiliated with the flight industry in any way, for what that's worth. With regard to any noises this light might have emanated (i.e., exhaust, sonic booms, etc.) from this aircraft, no discernible noise was noticed...the subject craft was the only aerial phenomenon noted in the southern sky at the time of the sighting and was so, for at least ten to fifteen minutes thereafter, before the local fireworks show/display began."

This orb was also witnessed by several people around him, and undoubtedly dozens more since it was at a firework exhibition. BR was straightforward and seemed to be very well educated as indicated by the lengthy four-page email with a detailed description of this aerial sighting.

MUFON Case: 77129

Location: Virginia Beach, Virginia

Date of Event: June 18, 2016

Date Submitted: June 18, 2016

Investigator: Norman Gagnon

On June 18, 2016, at approx. 9:55 p.m., "JP", along with another witness from a parking lot of a Virginia Beach store off 623 First Colonial Road, witnessed and videotaped several glowing red-orange orbs hovering at a distance over the area. The lights that were captured on video were slightly larger than the background stars and they seem to be flickering, perhaps due to the atmospheric turbulence (scintillation effect) or caused by the energy output from these UAPs.

JP was asked to describe what he witnessed. "We saw no more than 5 lights in formation moving from east to west (left to right on video) before disappearing. The sighting lasted 10 minutes, give or take. No jets were flying that day. Normally F/A 18 Hornets have flashing lights on the wings and rudders to aid in identifying each other and I did not see that."

Satellite imagery indicates that the Naval Air Station Oceana airport is just 2 miles south of where JP was videotaping. The orbs were hovering possibly very near or right over parts of the chance of the base personnel acknowledging this aerial incident with me would be unrealistic.

208

this airport and I would imagine that the base's personnel and perhaps the tower would have seen or picked them up on radar but

Conclusion:

So, how should we categorize these atmospheric phantom lights? They are spherical in shape, they radiate an intense fiery glow, comes in different sizes, and in some cases, they seem to be as curious of us as we are of them. Folklore and traditional legends from numerous countries and cultures have named them with such names as jack-o'-lantern, spook-lights, fairies, elemental spirits, Naga fireballs, and so forth. Skeptics explain them away as natural phenomena or photographic near-camera reflections of dust particles and the like.

As a paranormal investigator, it is my recommendation to keep a safe distance from these glowing spheres. However, with today's drone technology and their ever-increasing scientific capabilities, I believe that these unmanned aircraft systems/unmanned aerial vehicles (UAS/UAV) could be a tremendous tool to fly up close to these potential dangerous "orbs" as the drone's aerial sensors could detect temperature, density, and scan for other usable data, to determine if these glowing objects are solid in structure or pure energy, or perhaps a little of both. Of course, the stunning HD video footage that could be captured up close could be an added benefit as well!

Chapter Eight: William Dranginis – Monster Hunter
(January 18, 1959 – December 3, 2018)

Shortly after joining MUFON as a field investigator in 2004, I reached out to connect with other paranormal researchers and investigators in Virginia and further along the east coast. I soon found a gentleman who founded the Virginia Bigfoot Research Organization (VBRO). William (Bill) Dranginis has logged over 125 Bigfoot sightings since founding VBRO, many of which were in the southern Virginia area. After I introduced myself to Bill with an email, I expressed an interest in learning more about the elusive creature. He eagerly offered to assist me with my field research and to let me use his electronic gear if I ever need it.

Although our paths had crossed on a couple of occasions at the intersection of extraterrestrial and cryptozoology, we really didn't have the opportunity to actually work together on a case, sorry to say.

Norman Gagnon © 2010

Bill was knowledgeable with electronic detection devices and at the time we first started to share correspondences, he was employed with the Windermere Group in Annapolis, Maryland. There, he worked with search, guidance, navigation, and aeronautical systems. If you are familiar with James Bond's Q-Branch of MI6, Bill would be the real-life equivalent of "Q".

For a while, we frequently emailed each other and exchanged our respective investigative techniques. We discussed some of his new ideas on trying to suppress trail cameras from producing ultrasonic audio and infrared outputs; sounds and illumination outside a human's range of field but well within the range of most animals.

In jest, I suggested that he could invent a "Faraday Shield" aerosol so one could simply spray on electronic devices or even clothing to conceal these electronic emissions. Bill replied nonchalantly, "Oh, I'm working on that, Norm!"

Bill's idea behind this was to try to capture photographs or videos of the elusive Sasquatch or other man-beast-type creatures that roam our vast forests without having them "sense" these electronic devices that may drive them away. In 1997, Bill developed an experimental remote stealth camera decoy system that he called the 'EyeGotcha'. He custom-built these cameras and provided them to his network of professional hunters, law enforcement agencies, and branches of the United States military for 'test and feedback'.

He has also once corresponded with the world's foremost expert on chimpanzees, the English primatologist and anthropologist Jane Goodall. To me, it made sense to make contact with somebody who studied the behaviors and social interactions with wild species of primates.

Bill and I kept in contact for years before his death in 2018. As a memorial of sorts, I would like to share one of many emails we exchanged regarding the potential uses for electronic field equipment that he utilized in his monster hunts.

212

Here is an excerpt of an email exchange between Bill and myself on March 12, 2008.

"Hi Norm,

The most important use for Thermal Imaging technology in UFO research is to spot UFOs in the sky. I spotted a UFO while testing a FLIR (Forward Looking Infrared) camera at my home in Manassas. I was in the front yard checking out a new camera when I noticed a bright image near the horizon using the thermal camera. The object was moving fast and was coming directly towards my house. I could not see anything with my naked eye, but the thermal camera saw it as hot because it appeared bright white. That particular thermal camera did not display the subject's temperature, but the brightness of the object indicated it was really hot. The object went right over my house and I snapped a single frame picture of the round object. The object did not make any sound as it went overhead and did not have any lights. I have no doubt the thing was a UFO as I later took pictures of planes, birds, bats, and even bugs that had their own unique thermal signature. In other words, the plane looked like a plane, and the birds looked like birds, etc...

I have complete access to two handheld FLIR units I use at

work and was even instructed to take them home to use them so I stay current with their usage. I also have all the digital recording gear to save the video from them. The ultraviolet camcorder I also purchased for here at work can detect and record coronas around electrical poles and substations. I will be using this to see if the corona around UFOs that may be detected as I hear lots of stories about the objects being surrounded by blue light, this is very similar to the corona around electrical insulators. Heck, it's worth a shot, one never knows what may surface from the experimentation.

I did see the ghost group on TV using the FLIR units, but from the show, you see when they display the video on the TV, they don't know how to properly set up the camera, so they have no clue how to properly use the equipment. I learned all about the FLIR cameras when I completed the thermographer [thermal evaluator and imaging expert schooling] at FLIR in Boston, Mass.

I will be spending lots of time at my West Virginia cabin this summer looking for UFOs using the thermal and UV camera. There is a fire tower up there that provides 70-mile views, so that's the place to be. The location is also perfect for Bigfoot research.

I do have also access to a Crime Scope, which was when I purchased it while setting up the forensic lab here at work. I can also use that anytime I want. Now that is a piece of equipment that can be used for evaluating a past UFO landing spot. Many materials fluoresce if flooded with the right wavelength of light. So there are a number of ways to determine if something is left behind at a UFO landing site.

Let me know when you have the time so you can see how the equipment works…I have been using the UVCorder at the cabin to test different types of camouflage clothing, the equipment works really well."

April 2008 – Visit with Bill Dranginis in Manassas, Virginia

I finally had the opportunity to meet with Bill in the spring of 2008 when he invited me to his home in Manassas, Virginia. I was looking forward to talk with him in person when I drove up to his driveway and parked my car next to his house. As I looked at the dense forest behind his home, I thought of how rich in history the whole area is, especially when it comes to the Civil War.

As I stepped onto the porch, the front screen door swung open and Bill met me in the doorway with a big smile. After introducing me to his family, Bill and I went around the house to his backyard and into the woods.

He began to tell me about his first encounter with the Bigfoot that took place in Culpeper County near an old, abandoned gold mine that was about twenty miles southwest from where he lived.

While Bill and I walked, he shared his experience with me. In March 1995, Bill was with two FBI agent friends trying out a new White Eagle Spectrum metal detector in a large field at the edge of a wooded area near the abandoned gold mine. After a few hours of searching for Civil War artifacts, they headed back toward their vehicles via an old logging road. As Bill followed the agents, one stopped and said that he saw movement with his peripheral vision. He turned and saw a large creature standing upright trying to conceal itself behind some trees at the forest's edge. Instinctively, the agent drew his 9mm gun. This caught the attention of his two companions.

Turning toward the wooded area where the agent had his gun drawn, all three men saw movement, and then what appeared to be the head of some creature emerge. Almost immediately after being discovered, the creature slowly retreated behind the trees and ran into the forest. Bill knew immediately that what all three had seen was not human and it was not a black bear. Suddenly, the creature sprinted on its back legs swiftly down a hill away from the men. Bill estimated that the hair-covered humanoid was well over seven feet tall, which is the typical size of a Bigfoot.

Bill continued with his Bigfoot sighting story, "Norm, I still can see this creature in my mind's eye of what took place thirteen years ago…a 15-second sighting that I will never forget. I've since tried to find and photograph these Bigfoots. I'm glad that I had two other witnesses with me, especially both being Special Agents of the Federal Bureau of Investigation!"

As Bill and I walked further into his backyard, I approached what I really came to see. It was a heavily modified 24-foot 1989 Ford RV camper, affectionately referred to as his Bigfoot Primate Research Lab with a Virginia license plate that read VA YETI.

Virginia Bigfoot Research Organization (VBRO) Bigfoot Primate Research Lab

Bill had spent over $50,000 of his own money to "Q-outfit" this vehicle with state-of-the-art surveillance equipment.

A roof-mounted video camera with a 360-degree range, an aviation scanner to listen to airports airborne communications high above him, two night-vision cameras, a Forward-looking Infrared (FLIR) Imager, and a *Raytheon* NightSight 200 thermal camera on a 25-foot-tall telescopic mast. Being an RV camper, it also had a bed, bathroom, and shower for those extended field research expeditions.

After he gave me an overview of the RV, Bill opened a utility drawer and pulled out a few Bigfoot plaster footprint casts. He said that although he was satisfied with this collection, he was in the process of acquiring a plaster cast from the original Bigfoot mold made by Roger Patterson in Bluff Creek, California in 1967. Patterson is the man who made the Patterson-Gimlin 16mm film, which is perhaps the most famous piece of Bigfoot footage ever.

After Bill and I left the RV, we walked down a small incline to the entrance of a small grey garage that was nearby. Inside, the entire building was full of equipment placed on several shelves. I spotted a portable power supply and many pieces of electronic gear on his workbench. There were several stackable storage containers that overflowed with wires, connectors, cables, and power adapters. I noticed a microscope tucked away in the corner. Looking around in awe, on one wall I spotted a vintage color illustration that appeared to have been cut out from a magazine from the 1960s.

It was of an ape-like caveman atop a ravine throwing large stones toward horrified fur traders riding in a canoe down a river.

Bill and I chatted for a while before he excused himself for a moment. He returned with a VHS video cassette and showed me some amazing footage that he captured on one of his Bigfoot investigations in southern Virginia. I got the impression that not too many people had seen this footage. This video was taken late at night with a motion-detection, infrared video camera. He said that it was on the property of an unidentified witness where a few Bigfoot sightings had occurred. The camera was placed on the back porch of the witness's house facing the woods. Bill explained that he rigged up a long string tied to a rice cake as bait that was secured to a branch about twelve feet off the ground. While we were watching the video, he said, "Norm, keep an eye out to the left of the dangling rice cake."

A moment later, I suddenly saw a tiny arm reach for the rice cake. It stretched for the crispy morsel several times but it just could not make contact. The arm then retreated back and away from camera's range. Soon, a huge hairy forearm pierced through from the left side of the camera's range and easily grabbed the rice cake, instantaneously breaking the string before it retreated back into the shadows!

I was amazed. I said, "Wow, Bill! Why have I not seen this footage on local news or any of those Bigfoot documentaries? Bill replied, "I'm not ready to release this footage yet. I need to gather more evidence."

As the Manassas sky grew dim, Bill and I left the garage and walked to the side of the building. He pulled out a handheld FLIR imager from a bag and set the thermal palette to White Hot. He asked me to place my hand onto the surface of the garage and pull it away. I did so and he had me look at the imager. I looked through the display screen and saw my white heated handprint glowing brightly on the garage's weathered planks. I asked him about the difference between the FLIR imager and a set of night vision goggles.

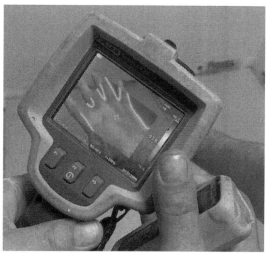

My hand under a current thermal imaging camera

Bill explained the difference. "The difference between a thermal imaging optic and a night vision enhancement device is that a thermal cam operates by sensing and capturing heat signatures from surfaces such as a warm body that would likely emit much more of a "white heat" than the cooler surroundings as to the ground, trees, or the garage surface that you just touched."

"Night vision goggles work by collecting the tiny amounts of light and amplifying it. The wearer will see everything in green because human eyes can distinguish more shades of green than any other color. In this case, your glowing handprint radiation transfer will eventually fade to grey and soon to black as it cools down."

I followed Bill back towards his house in total darkness and he began to share another Bigfoot story that took place in one of his cases. Suddenly, we both heard a series of high-pitched shrieks coming from nearby trees! I swear that it sounded like some chimpanzees were fighting above us...or it could have been a couple of young Sasquatches quarreling. Bill was startled too, but he soon realized that these screeches had come from some barn owls clashing overhead, perhaps over a freshly caught rodent. That was really an amazing meeting!

DNA Evidence

Bill and I kept in touch over the years. In the summer of

2011, he sent me an email with a link to an online post that he wrote in response to a critical thinking blog that he felt was leaning toward belittling most of the Bigfoot researchers and their investigative procedures. Here is the section from his reply to blog.

"Collecting stories and sightings has and will continue to be a very important part of this research. They provide a glimpse of what the witness observed during their chance encounter. It's possible that many sightings are just misidentifications of known animals or someone dressing up in a suit, but there are many sightings of the Bigfoot creatures that should not be cast aside. Many stories and sighting reports are very important tools to move this research forward. If you intend to improve on current procedures I would first advise that you evaluate many of the historical sightings and spend some time interviewing a number of the past and present-day researchers so you don't repeat history.

Has evidence improved over time? No. But I will bet you that there is already evidence of the creature's existence in museums scattered around the globe. Some of the scientists that work at these museums have no right to work there in the first place. I'm sure existing evidence of these creatures has been misidentified by the very people that claim to be experts in their fields. I know this for a fact as I went through the "scientific process" of having some possible Bigfoot hair tested. The hair was tested by "scientists" at the Smithsonian, then on to a PhD that conducted hair mineral analysis, then onto Seattle Washington for more hair identification testing then finally to having the hair tested for DNA by a world-class Laboratory. Guess what, the Smithsonian misidentified the hair, the hair mineral analysis was way off base, the two "expert" scientists that studied the hair in Seattle were wrong. It all came down to the DNA, the results indicated the hair came from a wolf. So you see, I followed the scientific process in reaching out to have the hair identified and unfortunately, all the so-called experts were dead wrong with their identification results. So just because a "scientific expert" puts their stamp on a piece of evidence, it may be something totally different. I do agree the scientific approach is the right way to go, but it's not always right.

Has physical evidence improved over time? Not really, but research techniques and technology have drastically improved over the last several years, as we gain more knowledge from fieldwork, we can combine new emerging technologies to help gather new evidence. This research has not been easy especially with the new television shows…Bigfoot creatures knocking on trees for communication or almost every call from the forest belongs to a Bigfoot creature, where is the evidence that proves that?

Bill wanted me to read his reply to this internet blog and to take what he wrote to heart. In the same email, Bill wrote, "Norm, keep this blog post in your field notes, you may use it on your S.E.A.R.C.H. website if you like."

Lake Champlain's Champ – Dranginis' Research Continues
Although Bill was well known for his investigations of Bigfoot, he also was interested in other creatures. One thing that he was particularly interested in was a water-creature believed to live in Lake Champlain, which is a 125-mile freshwater lake that borders on the states of Vermont and New York and the Canadian province of Québec (my old stomping grounds).

Over the years, there have been over 300 reported sightings of a lake creature that has become affectionately referred to as Champ. The first account of Champ was recorded in 1609 by Samuel de Champlain, the French explorer who founded *Québec* in 1608. Even before Champlain's account, several Native American tribes such as the Iroquois and Abenaki had their own run-ins with Champ, known to them as either 'Chaousarou' or 'Tatoskok'.

Until shortly before his death, Bill also worked with

defense-related contractors and as a senior science technologist at the Northrop Grumman Corporation in the Washington D.C. area. As a result, he had access to the latest emerging technologies from these companies, which in turn inspired him to devise ways to better detect and photograph these creatures without harming them. Mostly this had to do with identifying and photographing them with equipment that was outside a person's normal range of sight and sound.

Bill has traveled to Lake Champlain on numerous expeditions in the hopes of electronically capturing a recording of Champ. After thousands of hours of personal research, including examining a few videos taken by other researchers, Bill believed that there, in fact, may be some sort of unknown animal, possibly even a descendant of the plesiosaur, swimming beneath the surface of this expansive and frigid lake.

In his free time, Bill designed an underwater recording device that he called the EyeGotcha H20. It was a custom-built submergible device consisting of a 4-inch diameter PVC tube that housed a powerful video camera with hydrophones (microphones specifically designed to work underwater). The EyeGotcha H2O was powered by a rechargeable 12-volt battery. The PVC tube was painted bright yellow and the internal camera could reach a depth of approximately fifty feet. This device resembled today's aquatic side-scan sonars used by oceanographers and marine archaeologists to conduct underwater research. His prototype device was connected to a long polypropylene rope and to a large plastic buoy. He was able to use the EyeGotcha H2O several times with some success at Lake Champlain.

Photograph by Darrow Montgomery 2017

In the summer of 2017, Bill self-funded his own expedition of the Vermont coast of Lake Champlain and purchased a 31-foot boat for the adventure. He outfitted the vessel with his latest aquatic equipment in much the same way as the RV that I saw at his Virginia home. Now he was primed for the quest to discover the mysterious creature hidden beneath the surface of the lake.

Unfortunately, before he was able to go on this latest expedition with his new research boat, his exploration was cut short. On December 3, 2018, Bill Dranginis, who had been fighting pancreatic cancer, passed away at 59 years of age.

Bill, thank you very much for your research in this eccentric field and for sharing your findings with all of us. Rest in peace my friend.

With permission, I've added this tribute titled, 'The Spy Chasing Champ and Bigfoot' by Loren Coleman, December 3, 2018:

William "Bill" Dranginis, who had been fighting pancreatic cancer, passed away. He had moved to Florida, to be near his family, in the last few months. Bill Dranginis, age 59, was a surveillance and security expert, a consultant to the FBI and other agencies I can't reveal, who was originally from Manassas, Virginia.

In 1995, Bill had a sighting of a Bigfoot while metal detecting with intelligence community friends in the forests near Culpeper, Virginia, and had since then dedicated his free time and efforts to capturing video and audio evidence as proof of the creatures' existence.

Bill sold the Bigfoot Research vehicle to purchase a more

permanent Bigfoot research station in the hills of West Virginia. Bill was a highly respected researcher in the field and he created the "EyeGotcha" Digital Video surveillance system. This system is virtually sound-proof and can be deployed in the forests for long periods of time. The camera captured full motion video and audio that can be uploaded to a computer for later analysis. Bill felt it would be the break-through the Bigfoot field had waited for as far as the ability to capture video and audio of Bigfoot.

He also created a company to manufacture and sell the EyeGotcha camera systems. Bill was a FLIR Certified Level 1 Thermographer and has extensive knowledge with camouflage, concealment, and deception techniques. He also purchased surveillance watercraft and traveled to Lake Champlain to hunt for the "Monsters" there. His search for Champ, sadly, was running out of time. Bill was going to come to the International Cryptozoology Conference in 2018, to discuss his quests. But instead, we missed him deeply when he had to cancel due to his cancer. I talked with him often in the last months, and his death was a sad time for all of his friends and associates. Personally, I would like to thank Bill Dranginis, once again, for his donation of unbreakable, kid-friendly, nearly transparent two-part clear urethane display casts of the footprints of various hominoids, to the International Cryptozoology Museum.

It was great working with Bill on his educational projects. Dranginis's specially designed casts are a great resource invention. His sharing will live on, and the experiences he had with me. Bill was a thoughtful, thorough, and future-thinking researcher in cryptozoology. He will be missed.

Loren Coleman: Director International Cryptozoology Museum, and has been doing cryptozoology fieldwork since 1960, writing over 40 books and hundreds of articles since 1969, as well as being a documentary program and film consultant for decades.

In 2018, Animal Planet aired a new series called '*Extinct or Alive*' hosted by conservationist Forrest Galante, a man who travels around the globe to learn about possibly extinct animals. Midway through this episode, Forrest comments on his distinct type of clothing he was wearing that block the body's naturally occurring electrical energy signals. This made my ears perk up; while I remember joking about this fictional technology as I called it "Faraday shield aerosol" back in 2004 in the course of my emails exchange with Bill.

It would seem that this new EMR (electromagnetic radiation) textile blocking technology is upon us. I wanted to find out more about this new type of clothing, so I searched the internet and it revealed two men named Mike Slinkard and Max Maupin. They designed special hunting clothing back in 2010 that has electricity-conducting carbon woven into the grid pattern to block the electromagnetic field. The name of the company is HECS Hunting.

Most wildlife (and I assume Bigfoot as well) have an acute ability to hear, sense, and conceivably see electromagnetic patterns more successfully than the humans who are trying to be covert while sneaking around in the woods in camouflage clothing. The HECS clothing technology theoretically blocks most of the electrical energy radiation and preventing animals from sensing human presence. I believe that Bill was ahead of the game entailing this "cloaking" technology idea some 14 years prior, involving the potential capture of illusive creatures within their remote habitats on photographs. This is still an extraordinary step forward in learning more about these cryptozoological beasts.

Chapter Nine: No Matter How You Slice It

As Winston Churchill once said, *"It is a riddle, wrapped in a mystery, inside an enigma"*

In 2014, I wrote a lengthy adage of sorts for my Facebook page titled *Apple Slicer* that read:

"In the areas of paranormal/preternatural investigation, these fields of research often are separated and categorized into confined segments, as to an apple slicer, leaving behind the core. In my many years of research into the strange cases of ghostly activity, cryptic creatures, crop circles, and ufology, I have discovered that there seems to be a common thread that connects these phenomena, one of which would be the infamous orbs – an effortless pattern of energy; perchance waiting to transform into a shape based on your belief system. Perhaps we should not be too hasty to discard the core and focus on the seeds within." – Norman Gagnon 2014

Illustration by Norman Gagnon © 2014

Through my years of research, I have come across many reports from other field investigators that involve unearthly beings or strange anomalies that seem to have jumped over these "stainless steel barriers" and into another's domain. For example, there was a 2011 MUFON case I read from the database that involved a Burlington, Kentucky, woman who witnessed a seven-foot-tall humanoid-like primate with reddish hair. This creature appeared to have a translucent aura around it, glowing as it ran very quickly across her path and disappeared into the forest.

Was this humanoid a spirit manifestation, a Sasquatch chasing after its meal, or perhaps an alien scurrying back to its spacecraft? Who do you call to investigate this type of incident? Providentially, she submitted her report to the MUFON website (mufon.com) for our field investigators and members to peruse over.

Sometimes these types of high-strangeness sightings simply do not fit into a specific category within ufology, ghost hunting, or cryptozoology. Bear in mind that today's apple slicers also comes with 16 dividers, doubling the unearthly classifications from my illustration above.

If it looks like a duck, swims like a duck, and then it suddenly emits a wailing shriek as its feathers transform into turbulent flames, chances are that it is not really a duck. At this point, your deductive reasoning will have to take a short break, but the field investigators will still have to scribble down in their notebook the exact description as it is being observed or described to them.

In this chapter, you will experience a handful of cases I was directly involved with, that was stamped *"anomalous phenomena"*:

MUFON Case: 64920
Location: King George, Virginia
Date of Event: April 23, 2015
Date of Assignment: April 24, 2015
Investigator: Norman Gagnon

SYNOPSIS: The witness reported a large semi-transparent rectangular object with lights slowly hover across a highway.

ACCOUNT: On April 23, 2015, at 10:10 p.m. the witness initials "SM" was driving south on Route 301 when she noticed a large rectangular object in the sky with white lights in the front and rear. There was also a red light pulsing on the rear of the craft. She estimated that it took about three minutes to cross the highway and silently disappear into the distance as it hovered across the Virginia side of the Potomac River. As for the size, she felt that it was approximate twice the size of an American football field.

SM described her experience in detail. "It didn't appear to have much thickness from my perspective and I couldn't really see much of anything between the two rows of lights. I was seeing the lights mostly from underneath. It was more like a disturbance in the space between the rows of lights like it was distorted against the night sky full of stars, like watching a panel of glass float by. The lights on the front and the back remained perfectly equidistant from each other the entire time the object flew by…it floated very smoothly in a straight line from the right to left. It was definitely NOT two planes flying in sync with each other, which my rational mind was trying to make work as an explanation."

Illustration by Norman Gagnon © 2015

CORRELATING CASES:

According to the National UFO Reporting Center (NUFORC), a similar incident took place on April 20, 2015, in Cleveland, Oklahoma. A husband and wife witnessed a large rectangular craft with white lights in the same position as the Virginia encounter. They described it as a silent translucent rectangle that was larger than a football field. As with the Virginia sighting, the couple estimated that it took approximately two or three minutes to cross their point of view and fly into the distance.

MUFON Case: 65319
Location: Blackstone, Virginia
Date of Event: August 10, 1998
Date of Assignment: May 10, 2015
Investigator: Norman Gagnon

This interesting case comprised of a small hovering spherical object that was described as reflective and seen in the daylight. At approximately 10:00 a.m., KR was stationed at the Fort Pickett Army National Guard Base near the motor pool when he noticed the object hovering above the trucks. The Private estimated that the object was about 50 feet away from the trucks.

He reported that the sphere moved vertically and then horizontally before it disappeared. At first, the Private thought was, it was a bird but after he watched the object for a few moments he realized that it was a chrome sphere that silently move over the lot. When asked about the size he estimated that it was approximately five inches in diameter.

Illustration by Norman Gagnon © 2015

KR was asked to describe what he saw. "This object hovered for maybe five to six minutes with no sound and seemed to fade in and out of view as "it" realized I was on to it. The object moved side to side and as I moved closer to get a better look, it darted toward the front gate and just faded and disappeared!"

Soon after his encounter, Private First Class KR immediately went back into the building to look for his Section

Sergeant to tell her what he just saw. KR continued, "I'm really not sure why I didn't go grab her at first, I guess I was just amazed at what I was seeing and at the same time was in a state of disbelief. I had no sense of fear or anxiety associated with this event. Just a feeling of how cool this was and I had to tell someone quick!"

MUFON Case: 38470

Location: Falls Church, Virginia

Date of Event: May 15, 1989 – Historical

Date of Assignment: May 24, 2012

Investigator: Norman Gagnon

On Monday, May 15, 1989, at around 7:00 a.m., George a 62-year-old professional analyst was driving heading east on Columbia Pike/Route 244 in Falls Church, Virginia. As he waited at a traffic light across from the Barcroft Plaza Shopping Center, he glanced up and saw a large lenticular cloud that rapidly changed form. As George watched the dark grey cloud, it rapidly began to form into a spherical shape that he thought resembled some sort of 'craft'. Once the traffic light changed, George maintained eye contact for about a minute before the buildings and landscape obstructed his view. During an interview, George described the object. "I estimated the object to be approximately one to three miles away and at least the size of a football stadium. For the most part, the object was stationary, simply parked in the sky."

George said that although the object was motionless in the sky, it appeared to rotate and change shape. He described the object's first appearance as a classic saucer-shaped object with a smooth dark grey surface. Then, it rotated slightly to reveal a translucent and shiny rectangular bottom. Soon, George watched lines form around the top of the object that reminded him of a circular ring or halo.

As the interview progressed, George further described his experience. "Suddenly, a semi-circle of beautifully bright, red lights appeared flashing from right to left. The lights were separated and somewhat rectangular in shape with the narrow sides touching each other. The way these red lights flashed reminded me of some Ford Mustang's taillights. The thing that impressed me is the way the object just hung there, clearly owned the sky. It was methodical and behaved in an unhurried manner without any apparent concern. Unfortunately, shortly after the lights started flashing the traffic light change. I drove in the direction of the object and would get even a better view. After the road curved beyond the intersection in descending down to the lower elevation, and the object was never seen again."

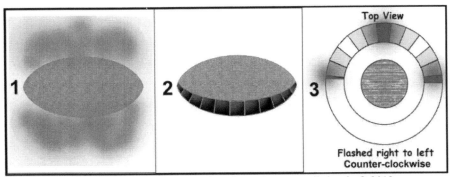

Illustration by Norman Gagnon based on witness pencil sketch. © 2012

I asked George why he waited 23 years to file his report with MUFON. He replied that it was not his intention to wait for so long, but he became busy with his career and family life. After several years, he became concerned that if he did not share his encounter sooner, that his account of the sighting could be lost.

This aerial anomaly that transformed above him reminds me of the previous case with Randy and Joyce that involved an UAP that changed into a *ringed unidentified object* hovering overhead as it changed or morphed into another shape. In both cases, the object exhibited an outer ring with an internal "porthole" that displayed yet another unidentified object.

MUFON Case: 58139

Location: Caret, Virginia

Date of Event: July 17, 2014

Date of Assignment: August 4, 2014

Investigators: Norman Gagnon, Phil Reynolds

On a few of my field investigations, I sometimes ask for another investigator to join me so we can cover more ground.

"MK" reported that on July 17, 2014, at approximately 10:20 p.m., he observed a bright, fiery diamond-shaped UAP over his property.

The main's witness' girlfriend "CD" filed the report with MUFON, yet the actual observer was her boyfriend MK. I asked fellow MUFON Field Investigator Phil Reynolds to assist me on this on-site investigation on the afternoon of July 20th, 2014.

CD and MK live in a house in a rural area off Store Road adjacent to his grandfather's residence. Upon our arrival, CD was holding her newborn, invited us into her home, and a few minutes later, MK (the witness) joined us in the living room. I asked him to show us where he was located during the sighting. We walked out the front door and onto the small porch where MK pointed to where he was sitting down. He said that he saw bright flashes from out of the corner of his eye to his left.

He turned his head and saw a brilliant orange diamond-shaped object swiftly descend behind some trees about 200 yards away.

The object traveled so fast that MK expected to hear the sound from an impact, but none occurred. MK added that he felt the heat from the object. MK was the only eyewitness to the phenomenon. Photos were taken from the porch from where the sighting took place. See the actual photograph with the added illustration below.

Left – actual backyard photo with illustration added by Norman Gagnon.
Right – myself with the witness. Photo by Phil Reynolds © 2014

We proceeded to walk toward the back of the property and as we passed the steel-roofed garage, MK added that on the night of the sighting he and CD were looking around their backyard. MK admitted that he felt as if something was watching him. Suddenly they both heard a loud clatter of something striking the steel garage. They both got frightened and ran back to the safety of their home. MK presented as a very credible and straightforward witness. He did not embellish or speculate about his sighting.

Reynolds and I searched the area where MK said that the UAP appeared above, looking for physical/trace evidence. I walked the tree line with MK and we saw no clearly identifiable traces from contact with any fallen airborne object. A few feet into the forest's edge, I saw a white oak tree. Upon looking closer, I noticed that on this one specific tree, the branches were full of welted leaves with multiple holes throughout its foliage. Leaves in this condition may be indicative of brief but intense heat exposure or perhaps from a disease or disorder, but the actual cause of this condition is uncertain. There were no visual/audible alerts from my EMF meter.

Information collected:

Photographs: Digital:

Canon SLR EOS Rebel XT 8.0 mpxl, SN# 0320141855, 18-55mm lens, SN# 9700503763

Nikon Coolpix S3000 12.0 mpxl, SN# 38609775

Geiger Counter: Model DV-715, SN# 278285 – on setting "X100"

Result: Negative

Bendix Dosimeter: Model CD V-742, SN# 0730553 – Result: Negative – needle remained on zero, indicating no exposure.

TriField EMF Meter: Model 100XE – on setting "Magnetic (0-3range)"

Result: Set to alert on any reading: No alert.

MUFON CASE# 74871

Location: Prince George, Virginia

Date of Event: Feb 29, 2016

Date of Assignment: Mar 01, 2016

Investigator: Norman Gagnon

In February of 2016, at about 11:45 a.m., a Virginia man in his mid-50s, named "Cliff", sauntered back from The Crossings Shopping Center after a quick bite, as he has done many times during his lunch hour over the years. However, on this day something above him caught his attention.

Cliff is working directly with the Department of Defense and has a Top-Secret clearance. He is a former United States Marine scout sniper, Huey helicopter crew chief, and field engineer. He also has a Bachelor of Science in aviation maintenance and a Master's degree in software engineering. I believe he would be a qualified observer, to say the least.

Cliff's report about his experience indicated that as he turned his head northeast toward Jefferson Park Road, his attention was drawn upward by a strange sickle-shaped object that simply floated above the tree line a few yards away. The surface of this object was overall silver with a small, highly reflective oval-shaped feature on the upper part of this mysterious vehicle. At first, Cliff thought it was a kite but after a few moments, he realized that it was motionless.

Per my request, Cliff provided a sketch of what he saw that morning of which I recreated in an illustration. Please note the similarity of this drawing to the UFO sketch by pilot Kenneth Arnold that he witnessed on June 24, 1947, in Washington State.

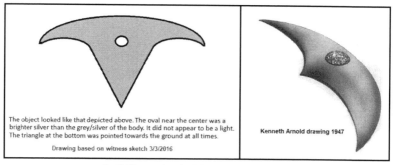

The object looked like that depicted above. The oval near the center was a brighter silver than the grey/silver of the body. It did not appear to be a light. The triangle at the bottom was pointed towards the ground at all times.

Drawing based on witness sketch 3/3/2016

Kenneth Arnold drawing 1947

Left illustration by Norman Gagnon 2016

Cliff was asked to describe the object. "As I put in my initial report, I thought it was a kite when I first observed it. However, there was no lateral motion that you would normally see with a kite as it sways with the wind. This object was steady holding in one spot." He estimated that the object was approximately 30 feet in diameter. Cliff watched the stationary unidentified object for about a minute before it shot straight up into the sky.

Cliff did not believe that this was a drone because the upward lift was much faster than any aircraft he has ever seen. Cliff, "This object was steady holding in one spot before going straight up and out of sight...not behind clouds mind you, just straight up into the open sky. I have a lot of experience with drones. I was part of the development and fielding efforts for Global Hawk and Predator. I also observed the small Drones used by my Marines in Iraq in 2004 and programs such as Global Hawk, Predator, Hunter, EMALS, and more."

When asked about whether the object made any sound, Cliff said that he was too far away to hear anything emanating from it. He added that he did not see anyone else in his vicinity during the time of the sighting.

Jellyfish Anomaly, Summer of 2003
My personal experience

This report is my own personal experience.
Two strange, identical objects that both my wife and I saw hovering in the sky while we were driving.
We just didn't know what these things were, so they were really unidentifiable.

On a beautiful afternoon, my wife and I were driving easterly on the Franconia-Springfield Parkway (Route 289), in Springfield, Virginia. The car windows were down as we enjoyed the warm breeze. Then to my left and overhead, I saw something that caught my attention. At first, I thought they were a couple of clouds floating above a few hundred feet in the air. I continued to look and then thought that they appeared to be hot air balloons. However, unlike most balloons that have vibrant colors, these were a dull grey and almost vaporous. I asked my wife to look at these strange things and she could not make sense of what they were, either.

Photo of Route 289. Added illustration by Norman Gagnon © 2020

Description of these bizarre aerial objects:

The pair of objects were identical in size and shape. They were both grey but appeared to be translucent, but dense enough to cast a shadow. Their tops were dome-like as their contour came into a point at their bases. At first, I described them as hot air balloons but they did not have large baskets attached at their bottoms, and surely they were not brilliant white high-altitude balloons as they were not transporting scientific payloads from connected lines.

I added this case to my AOL Hometown's S.E.A.R.C.H. website at that time and my wife and I chose to call these strange things "jellyfish objects".

This particular case caught the attention of a few paranormal field researchers and later I discovered that my SEARCH 'jellyfish objects' report was published in their 2007 book titled 'Weird Virginia' by Jeff Bahr, Troy Taylor, and Loren Coleman; on page 78 titled 'Jellyfish UFOs'.

MUFON Case: 34904

Location: Partlow, Virginia

Date of Event: January 3, 2012

Date of Assignment: January 22, 2012

Investigator: Norman Gagnon

This high-strangeness case is a good example of my "apple slicer" analogy on page 231.

On the night of January 3, 2012, a husband and wife (I will refer to them by their first names, Randy and Joyce) witnessed a bright circular light over their property away from their home. They got into their vehicle and drove to the location of the light, but since the light moved this soon led to a pursuit. Randy and Joyce decided to contact MUFON about their high strangeness experience and I was given the case to investigate.

I met with Randy and Joyce in their home at 11:00 a.m. on

January 27, 2012. Joyce and Randy live on a 20-acre property in the country outside of Partlow, Virginia. After we introduced ourselves, I decided to interview Joyce first. She told me that around 6:45 p.m. she arrived home and drove up the gated entrance on their property. There she noticed a bright pulsating light hovering a few yards over their property. At first, she thought that the light came from either a medivac or life-flight helicopter en route to a hospital. However, she soon realized that the object was silent.

Joyce returned to her carport and parked her vehicle. She entered the house and immediately told her husband about the strange hovering light. Randy rushed outside to investigate and saw that the light had moved closer to the backyard. The winter sun was setting by this time, so Randy hurried back into the house to get his spotlight. I asked him about his dogs' reaction to this UFO and he said that they remained quiet and apparently were undisturbed by this hovering anomaly.

At this point of the interview, she said that Randy went into his house and got his one-million candle power rechargeable spotlight to show to me. He said that he first signaled the UFO with this spotlight, which he estimated to be about 800 yards away and about 20 feet off the ground. He said that he flashed his spotlight on/off three times. When he did this, the UFO's brightness dimmed significantly for a few seconds before returning to its full intensity. Randy moved to a different part of his backyard to get a better look at the light. Again, he turned the spotlight on and off three times. As before, the UFO dimmed for a moment then became bright again

Randy carefully walked closer to the mysterious light but was abruptly stopped by what he described as a dark brown 'ghostly streak' that unexpectedly whooshed in front of him. It blocked his path for a few seconds and caused him to jump back a little. As Randy regained his composure, he took a few steps back towards his house and noticed a large shadow being cast across his lawn. He immediately looked up and saw a large rectangular object block out the moonlight as it hovered above him.

Randy was perplexed by the barrage of strange apparitions and felt as if the light source was trying to distract or misdirect him for an unknown purpose. However, but he was determined to find the source of this UFO as it began to move away from above his property. He ran into the house to get his wife Joyce and they got into their car to follow the object as it silently drifted westward.

At this point, I asked Randy and Joyce to retrace the path that they drove during their pursuit of this enigmatic light. We walked to their parked white 2011 Ford Taurus and I sat in the back seat. Joyce shared her perspective of the events that took place during the chase. She said that as they left their driveway, the car's center console started to generate a crackling, high-pitched static that lasted about thirty seconds. She added that this was the first and last time they ever heard the bizarre noise. I thought to myself, "I'm wondering if this entity was trying to communicate with them through the car's audio system in a similar fashion as to those 'spirit boxes' that are used by ghost hunters?"

As we proceeded down the main road about four miles from their house, Randy pointed to a cornfield on the left side of the roadway and said that this is where he and his wife both saw a man standing next to his car parked alongside the road. Apparently, the man may also have seen something very strange above him and pulled over to the side of the road to watch it. Looking at me from his rearview mirror, Randy said, "This guy was just standing there in a trance next to his red Ford Taurus with his head looking up at the sky, oblivious to us. He just kept looking up frozen as we drove by."

Not far from the area where they had seen the man, we made a slight right onto Edenton Road. Randy told me that this was the spot where he almost hit a coyote that ran in front of their vehicle while he pursued the lights.

Shortly after turning onto the Edenton Road, we pulled over to view an empty field that had a row of small pine trees about 150 yards from the road with a large wooden area further behind. While Joyce stayed in the car, Randy and I walked a few feet toward the young pine trees. He pointed to a modern Colonial-style house and said that he saw the anomaly floating near it.

Randy continued, "That night, we both saw the white house with a black roof and window shutters. It was easily seen in the bright moonlight. The bright light was to the left of the house and further back just above the trees. I took my spotlight and flashed at it a third time. It dimmed down but as it became brighter again, it changed shape into a large bluish-white glowing ring that had an oval disc at its center and this disc did reflect the moonlight as well. A few seconds later, the ring disappeared!"

He added that shortly after he saw the ring 'window' that revealed the UFO and a few seconds later it disappeared. Shortly after, the unidentified light reappeared in its original form but to the right of the house, and once again it was on the move! Randy and Joyce jumped back into their car and followed the moving light for approximately another six miles before they got tired of chasing it, made a U-turn, and drove back. Randy said, "Before we returned to our home, I checked the odometer reading and the total distance we traveled one-way was 10.4 miles."

Phantom House

Both Randy and Joyce have taken the same route to revisit the site a couple of times where they initially saw the ring-shaped portal. They both have also looked for the Colonial-style house to get a reference point of where they were that evening, but it simply wasn't there. They both remember seeing a light-colored two-story house with a black roof and shutters that fateful night but have since been unable to locate it again.

As for the main witness Randy, the mysterious light threw a handful of bizarre manifestations at him and even what may have been holographic projections, but for what purpose? Coyote sightings are somewhat rare in northern Virginia but was this animal that cut him off on the road, a "projection" or diversion to slow Randy down from chasing after this light?

So I have to ask, signaling or attempting to communicate with an unknown entity, and in the case of Randy with his spotlight, was this a precarious thing to do? This gesture seemed to have released outlandish manifestations directed at him. I also wondered about the man standing outside his car in a trance staring at the sky. Did he experience "missing time"?

Let's leap over another of these slicer barriers and into the realm of the supernatural. Below are two interesting encounters I personally experienced. This is a classification that very few paranormal authors will write about these days, perhaps because it is not a subject matter that promotes thrill, chill, or terror, but rather "uplifts one's spirit" if you will, a phenomenon that may divert one to a much-improved path in one life's journey…at least in my very own inexplicable travels. The subject is miracles.

Divine Intervention – Fall of 1987
My personal experience

One late afternoon in Alexandria, Virginia I was driving my brand new '88 Chevy Beretta CL with my friend Preston in the passenger seat, listening to some tunes. I took the Duke Street off-ramp and stopped at a traffic light, waiting to make a left turn onto North Van Dorn Street. A vehicle on my right also stopped to make this left turn as well. After what felt like forever, the light finally turned green. I pressed the accelerator pedal, but the engine simply died. Embarrassed by this being a new car I tried to quickly restart my engine, but the ignition would not turn over. The person in the vehicle behind me blew their horn, as the car next to me moved forward and proceeded to make a left turn. Suddenly, there was a loud crash followed by a shower of metal and glass fragments! I watched as the car that had been next to me a moment before being hit full force by another vehicle that had run through the adjacent red light.

Both Preston and I were shocked by what we just witnessed.

I tried to start my car again and the engine turned over smoothly and with no issue. I made my left turn and carefully drove around the accident. My tires crackled over the broken debris and in my rear-view mirror, I watched both drivers get out of their damaged vehicles. Although their vehicles looked to be totaled, both drivers appeared to be uninjured. I drove a few yards and turned into a plaza parking lot and parked my Berretta. I had to take a few moments to catch my breath and contemplate what had just taken place. Preston and I were both incredibly grateful that we were 'protected' from this dangerous accident by some unseen but undeniable force.

On a Wing and a Prayer – Summer of 2007
My personal experience

Now, here is n wondrous incident that I experienced in the late summer of 2007 in Springfield, Virginia that involved a vagrant man who tried to attack me. One mild afternoon I decided to walk from work to meet with my wife for dinner at a nearby restaurant. I cut through an industrial park and onto VA 617 South. I remained on the left side of a four-lane road, following a thin dirt path to a railroad bridge on the way to the restaurant. When I got close to the bridge, my path was blocked by a man on his hands and knees on top of a flattened cardboard box. As I carefully stepped off the path and quickly onto the traffic lane to walk around him, he immediately swung his head. His pale grey eyes met mine and he unexpectedly let out a loud growl! The man then got up, picked up his crushed box, and rushed away in the opposite direction.

I was disturbed by what I saw but continued walking up the incline of the bridge. I looked closely at the bridge and noticed how low the bridge's tubular railing fence was; I estimated that it was no higher than 36 inches at most. I looked over the bridge and thought that the railing was not much of a barrier from what seemed to be an 80-foot drop to the railroad tracks below. About halfway across the bridge, I had the strong feeling to turn around to check up on the poor soul who had growled at me a minute ago. I turned around and was surprised to discover that the man was running in full charge to attack me!

As the snarling man came closer, he suddenly stopped just a few feet away from me. We made eye contact again for just a few seconds, but he then looked up and over my shoulders. His face instantly changed from a scowl of anger to one of sheer fright. The man whirled around and ran away screaming!

I was a bit stunned by what had just taken place, but I turned back around and crossed the bridge to continue on my way to meet my wife. As I cut through the parking lot of a local burger joint, a yellow express delivery van with bright red letters stopped right next to me. The courier rolled down his window and asked me, "What the hell happened back there? This guy looked like he saw a ghost!" I thought for a few seconds and replied, "I think it was something much more frightening."

What I believe the drifter had witnessed was a very tall angelic being standing directly behind me, with its wings fully extended outward. I distinctively saw his grey eyes look way above my head prior to running away. Then I knew what protected me from either being pushed over the railing and down to the tracks below or shoved into oncoming traffic. This failed assault was quickly spoiled as it was also witnessed by a courier in his express van.

I met up with my wife about thirty minutes later. As we sat down at the restaurant's table, I shared my remarkable encounter with her as she was amazed and very glad I was safe.

■■■

"String theory envisions a multiverse in which our universe is one slice of bread in a big cosmic loaf. The other slices would be displaced from ours in some extra dimension of space."   - Brian Greene

In the 2002 book '*Lights in the Sky & Little Green Men*' by Hugh Ross, Kenneth Samples, Mark Clark, chapter 11, H. Ross wrote:

> "The universality of residual UFOs (RUFOS) in the human context can be expressed in a different way: UFOs change with one's to perceive them. UFO researcher Whitley Strieber noted that "the fifteenth century saw the visitors as fairies. The tenth century saw them as sylphs. The Romans saw them as wood-nymphs and sprites."

> "Today, human civilization presents a panoply of cultures and beliefs that constantly interact with one another. As one witness who had observed many different UFOs throughout his life stated…whatever cosmology or mythology I was immersed in seemed to be the factor for shaping the context and attendant imagery of my experiences."

In this day and age, specifically what appears to be "nuts & bolts" flying objects from just the last 60 years alone, seems to be keeping pace with our human technology and often mimicking the style and design of our Hollywood spacecraft from current blockbuster movies. Almost as if these mysterious airborne anomalies (or the unseen force behind them) are aware of what we're thinking; the capacity for UAP manifestations to adapt so well to the state of mind of the observer.

Here's a quote from Chapter Five of Dr. Jacques Vallee's book 'Dimensions – A Casebook of Alien Contact' that seems to put it all together.

> "Is it reasonable to draw a parallel between religious apparitions, the fairy-faith, the reports of dwarf-like beings with supernatural powers, the airship tales in the United States in the last century, and the present stories of UFO landings?"

Now, what about the discarded core that the apple slicer relinquished from its center that is merely tossed away to be forgotten? What is really the source behind the "seeds" that are planted deep into the subconscious of humankind that often and unexpectedly springs to life in the most extraordinary apparitions? I will leave this up to the readers to decide.

Chapter Ten: Modus Operandi

"My life seemed to be a series of events and accidents. Yet when I look back, I see a pattern." – Benoît B. Mandelbrot

Years ago, in my early twenties, I took a security job with the Wells Fargo Guard Services agency. Upon completion of the state training, and with the uniform, badge, and related gear, all of the security officers were given a small blue handbook that contained an important catchphrase written in the first chapter: *Observe and Report.*

An investigator, be it a journalist, police detective, or field researcher must always be aware of their surroundings. They also must have up-to-date skills in communication, interviewing techniques, and related tools for their research. An investigator will gather information from as many sources as necessary to get the facts and evidence that will often reveal the 'modus operandi' (M.O.) or method of operation in a case.

Adding the term 'paranormal' to the mixing bowl of an investigation is where things may become a bit problematic. Critical thinking is a great skill to have, but in field investigation, one must have an open mind to all possible explanations for extraordinary circumstances. Using the word paranormal may lend bias to an investigation by assuming that there may not be a rational explanation for an event. Sometimes a shadow is just a shadow.

Here are a few of the extraordinary accounts I chose to add to this chapter so you'll get a sense of my "method of operation" in the field of gathering information and reporting what you have seen.

September 11, 2001- Pentagon Attack
My personal experience

In 2001 I worked for the Computer Sciences Corporation within their Consolidated Support Facilities group which accommodated personnel related to the Department of Defense's Ballistic Missile Defense Organization (BMDO). Our team occupied a little more than half a floor of an undisclosed Crystal City (Arlington, VA) building only a few blocks south of the Pentagon. Although I did not know it at the time, there was another company that was about to occupy the other half of our floor...Gray Hawk Systems, a classified supplier of military equipment and special tactical gear for our U.S. elite ground forces.

On September 11, 2001 at 9:37 a.m. I felt a tremor in our

building and before long I saw several people running past my office door. A moment later our building fire alarm was activated, although I had no idea why at the time. I walked out of my office and looked through the north conference room windows. There I saw dark grey smoke billowing from behind some nearby buildings. Curious, I took the stairwell down a few flights to the Crystal City Underground Shops. I ran into the Rite Aid pharmacy and purchased a disposable 35mm camera because I had a gut feeling that this was more than a fire drill.

A few minutes later, I quickly exited the office building onto South Bell Street. This is when I first noticed that the street was full of motionless cars. Next, I saw a man in a suit with a circular badge with star on his lapel that appear to be directing traffic. He was from the U.S. Marshal Service as their office was located about a block south of my building. I started to walk toward the thickening dark plumes of smoke as I took several photographs.

On South Fern Street, I walked past the open rear door of Nell's Carryout Shack and overheard on their radio that the Twin Towers of the World Trade Center in New York City had been hit by airplanes. It was at this moment that I realized that we were under attack. I continued toward the smoke and meandered through a horde of incoming military personnel rushing away from the Pentagon. When I arrived at the edge of Interstate I-395, I saw that a crowd of people had gathered on my side of the highway for safety. There were a few emergency vehicles positioned on the street near the underpass.

Suddenly, another loud blast was heard. I thought it was a bomb explosion but in retrospect, I realized that the sound came from the Pentagon's roof collapsing from the intense fire. To my left, I saw a woman in a military uniform ran past me and yelling to the crowd of people that there was another airplane on its way and we must leave the area immediately! I thought to myself, "Really, Run where?"

Trying to understand what was happening, and as I walked a few yards toward the highway's guardrail, everything around me felt surreal.

There, I came upon a Pentagon construction worker wearing a red hardhat. We talked for a few moments. He explained that just a few minutes before the explosion, he left the Pentagon to go to his truck to gather some equipment and to have a cup of coffee.

While the construction worker was outside the Pentagon's perimeter, he saw an airliner fly really low, barely missing the Navy Annex building. It clipped a few parking lot's light poles before crashing into the side of the Pentagon! I realized that if this worker had not exited the Pentagon when he did, he may have died in this explosion from the 200,000-pound aircraft that impacted the area in which he had been working.

I wished him the best and continued walking on the grassy area next to the I-395 guardrail.

A few yards ahead, a group of Marine sergeants and a few officers had gathered in a circle. One Marine was recounting that he had also seen the plane hit the Pentagon. *Click...wind*, another photo taken. Not long after, I heard the roar of an F-16 Fighting Falcon fly over the Pentagon. It circled over the area a few times as if it was waiting to intercept another hijacked airliner. I snapped another photo.

Norman Gagnon 9/11/2001

I decided that I needed to return to my office building to contact my wife to let her know that I was alright. I soon found that none of the landline phones worked as to my cell phone because the entire system had collapsed, but despite that chaos that surrounded me, I was eventually able to make it home.

A decade later or so, a Discovery Channel special on 9/11 interviewed the pilot of the very same F-16 that flew over the Pentagon, which was First Lieutenant Heather 'Lucky' Penney. She and other pilots had been given the orders to take down the fourth plane before it reached Washington D.C. In her case there was not enough time to outfit her aircraft with live ammunition, so she was essentially on a suicide mission to ram into Flight 93! About an hour of being airborne, First Lieutenant Penney received the call that Flight 93 had crashed into a field in western Pennsylvania. So, after her flyover of D.C., she returned to Andrews Air Force Base safe and sound.

Within a week of 9/11, conspiracy theorists were online making posts on every social media outlet proposing grandiose assertions of what 'really' caused the Pentagon blast. Some believed that high-level government officials planned the attack. Others believed that American Airlines Flight 77 did not impact the Pentagon but rather asserted that it was hit by a satellite-guided missile. There were several other theories that had no basis on reality. Over twenty years later people still believe that 9/11 was an inside job. And here we go…anytime there is a historic event that changes our lives some people have difficulty accepting things as they are.

<u>May 7, 2012 – Knock, knock, who's there?</u>

<u>My personal experience</u>

In May of 2012, I accepted a short-term assignment at a historical building in Washington D.C. as a Facility Manager that provided on-site living accommodations. This place is a well-known non-profit charitable foundation. By the way, I was also within walking distance from a variety of great restaurants, coffee shops, and bookstores, an amazing locality to explore.

This 13,300 square foot, the four-story brick residence is located in the prominent 16th Street NW Historic District, built at the turn of the nineteenth century. I, being the new "caretaker" of this 104-year-old structure, expected the usual creaks, knocks, and groans noises from the building's continual expansion, contraction, along with the eerie clatter from the old plumbing fixtures. I also worked closely with the foundation's architect as this longstanding building was going through a handful of modernization projects. This dwelling also had slightly hidden doors that opened into an undersized servant staircase that covertly led to the other floors.

I do not want to reveal too many details that might disclose this location, but here's the short history of this home's occupants: Built for a Rear Admiral in the US Navy in 1908 and after, a doctor/professor that taught at the George Washington University purchased this home in 1943. A cult-like religious leader and proclaimed doctor of metaphysical science have both rented part of this building from this owner in the 1950s.

There were two strange episodes that took place during the four months I had spent at the house. I do not believe that my carpentry skills would have been able to fix these singularities.

The first incident took place after the end of my first day after I had completely secured all of the doors and turned on the security system. At approximately 11:30 p.m. as I was preparing to go to bed, the building's fire alarm sounded! I jumped off the bed and ran to the alarm control panel to see which smoke detector was activated. The display panel directed me to the first-floor hall next to the small elevator. I ran down the hall and thank goodness, there was no smoke in this area. Then as I looked up to the ceiling's smoke detector and unexpectedly, it was entirely covered with a swarm of tiny black flies! These insects apparently interrupted the sensor that activated the fire alarm. My first thought is to get rid of these flies so I went into the nearby closet and grabbed a bottle of window cleaner and squeezed a few blasts until they all dropped like, well…flies. Next, I waited for the DCFD Fire Department to arrive and to greet them with the front door wide open, (no axes needed thank you very much).

Two questions I still ask myself today: "Where did hundreds of flies come from and why were they drawn or lured to this one smoke detector?"

The second spooky occurrence took place a few weeks later while I was in my first-floor office late in the evening, around 10:30 p.m. Suddenly, I heard three loud knocks from what sounded like a brass knocker at the front door. I walked towards the entrance and slid the curtain to see through the glass but there was no one standing there. I deactivated the alarm and opened the door to look at the walkway but I did not see anyone in the area. I guessed then that this was the result of a prankster.

I decided next to go over the entrance camera recording to see if I captured this intruder on video. From my computer, I reviewed the security video footage to fifteen minutes prior to the knocks. I then examined the video carefully to look for the perpetrator that walked up to the front door but nothing was on video except when I opened the door! Incidentally, the front door does not have a door knocker, just a doorbell.

During the remainder of the four months of my temporary assignment, the building stayed rather quiet, or should I say, preternatural free. I got to thinking of the previous building manager and why he left this building, could it be that these paranormal incidents were a little too much for my predecessor?

On the bright side, during my last week at this site, the foundation invited several Muslim dignitaries to celebrate the final evening of Ramadan with a large fast-breaking meal. As I coordinated with the caterers who were preparing the Iftar dinner, one of the foundation's director ask me join him at the dining table which I gladly accepted. The caterers had the table set with a variety of authentic dishes from lentils-beef stew called Mawmenye, Moroccan Ksra and Harira vegetable soup, Khoresh Fesenjan, with other delicious spicy dishes, and of course a whole roasted lamb!

Now, how many ghost hunters out there would have loved to live in this century year old haunted house for sixteen weeks?

Secret Underground Compound
July 2012 – Washington, D.C.
My personal experience

In July 2012, I accepted a temporary assignment in Washington D.C. for approximately six months. During the first weekend of the relocation, my urban exploration sense and wanderlust kicked in, and being in the middle of Washington, D.C., there were countless places that I could explore and photograph. However, I decided to conduct a little internet search to check out the local 'urbex menu' within this historic city.

For those who don't know, 'urbex' is short for 'urban exploration', which entails exploring abandoned manmade structures or environments that often includes searching deserted buildings, factories, underground tunnels, decommissioned military installations, etc.

After looking online for a while, one particular location captured my attention. I found a 2004 article from *The Washington Post* about a secret compound built by the Naval Department that was hiding in "plain sight" on federal parkland. This site wasn't exactly abandoned but rather a newly built "secretive" hangar-like structure that the Navy Department simply took over from the National Park Service land. Personnel from The US Park Police Station were located just a few yards away were a bit troubled by this unannounced construction project.

After looking at a Google satellite image of the area, I realized that this location was located off of East Potomac Park about a quarter-mile south of the Jefferson Memorial.

The guard station with its multiple cameras. The NRG
are my initials.   Photo by Norman Gagnon © 2012

The Saturday after I learned about the compound, I dressed
as a visiting tourist with a colorful t-shirt, baseball cap, and digital
camera. I pulled into a somewhat empty parking lot and walked
under a railway bridge toward the entrance. Soon I made a left into
a driveway and came upon a gate. I made certain that I appeared
lost and frequently looked down at a tourist map. As I approached
the gate, I paid particular attention to the five security cameras
mounted at the upper left roof corner of the tan guard station. I
waited about thirty seconds for a security guard to quickly exit the
front door of this station and to escort me off the property, but the
door remained closed.

So, I began to take photos with my digital camera of the complex.

My view was hindered by a ten-foot wooden fence or barrier that surrounded the whole complex. I walked to the right of the guard's station for a few yards and found a large grey self-enclosed dumpster near the fence. I climbed on top of it to have a better view and I took a couple of photographs. A few seconds later I quickly jumped off the dumpster. I reviewed my digital pictures and noticed that the yard had a crane truck and other large-scale type equipment. It appeared that this may be the final phase of its construction, and also noted how large the warehouse doors were.

I continued to walk the perimeter of the fence and came upon a recessed area that had more construction equipment right across from the US Park Police Station. I looked at my surroundings and noticed a rather wide gap between two vertical boards in the wooden fence.

Without hesitation, I decided to peek through the opening. There was an older man in his late-sixties wearing thick orange coveralls with reflective tape and a yellow hardhat. He faced a tan storage building and appeared to be doing some sort of repair to it. I thought to myself how he was excessively dressed for light maintenance on a very hot day. I spun around to check on the Park Police building. I wanted to make certain that I did not attract the attention of the officers.

I decided it was time to backtrack past the guard station and under the railway bridge toward NW Parking Lot C. This was a lot reserved for construction personnel that I believe worked in this secret complex. I noticed that there was a Clark/Kiewit parking permit sticker on one of the parked vehicles' windshields. The construction crew for this compound was Clark Construction as the general contracting company and Kiewit Infrastructure as the mining and [tunneling] engineering company, which was very interesting. Is this a concealed hangar (gateway) to an underground tunnel or complex?

274

A 2009 timestamped Google Street view of this complex entrance revealed a few construction trucks transporting heavy equipment under a tarp. Another image showed a dump truck full of dirt exiting the compound. Further internet research revealed that there was a similar compound with tan buildings of identical architectural design in Austin, Texas. In both cases, the compounds were located close to railroad tracks. After doing extensive internet research, I believe that these large tan structures could be associated with the Federal Emergency Management Agency (FEMA) and that there are several such covert facilities located throughout the United States.

Underground Rails

Most high-ranking Washingtonians use a network of restricted underground rails beneath the city of Washington D.C called the U.S. Capitol Subway System. The system is only accessible to members of Congress and approved guests. These privileged people movers are located within the United States Capitol Building and connect the Senate and House office buildings.

MUFON Case: 57368

Location: Front Royal, Virginia

Date of Event: June 24, 2012

Date of Assignment: August 25, 2013

Investigators: Norman Gagnon (STAR FI), Phil Reynolds, Victor Rodriguez

Space Debris – Forest Fire

Background Environment:

In late June 2012, the U.S. Forest Service fought a wildfire that burned over 1,100 acres through Massanutten Mountain between Sherman Gap and Veach Gap, spanning both Shenandoah and Warren Counties. This mountain range parallels Interstate I-81, located about 10 miles southwest of Front Royal, Virginia.

I added this case to this chapter to give you, the readers, an idea of what an investigator will often go through to get even the most accurate hands-on information available to complete an investigation. In this instance, I was part of a team that investigated an incident of what may be described as 'space debris' that crashed and ignited the large forest fire in Massanutten Mountain, Virginia. In this particular case, the overall report/account consisted of four phases:

1) Space Debris or UFO Crash? (Who, what where, when and how)
   Review photos? Newspaper reports, Videos, etc.
2) Contact/email Fire Department, U.S. Forest Service, witnesses, etc.
3) In-person testimonies, follow-up interviews, on-site investigation
4) Submit individual reports; final report written by FI Victor Rodriguez

Days later, Victor gave me a digital copy of a photograph to analyze, that was emailed to him. A fiery object purportedly was captured in this digital photo. Based on the EXIF Viewer metadata results, the photo was taken the night of June 24, 2012, at 11:12 p.m., assumedly above this mountain range. However, the photo depicted a reddish crescent-shaped, indistinct object in an overall black environment, so this object could be anything.

EXIF (Exchangeable Image File Format) is the data that provides details about the image's properties. This file defines specific information related to an image or other media captured by a digital camera as in GPS location with latitude/longitude, date/time the image was captured, etc.

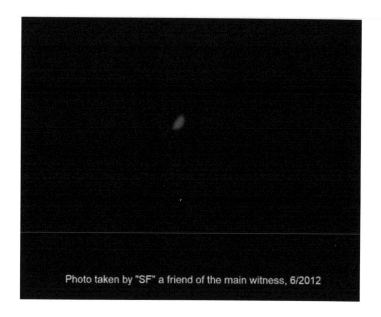

Photo taken by "SF" a friend of the main witness, 6/2012

I wanted to discover the source of the fire but it was difficult to gather the facts. Some of the information gathered came through Freedom of Information Act (FOIA) requests submitted to both the U.S. Forest Service (USFS) and North American Air Defense Command (NORAD). Only the USFS replied to our inquiry about the possibility of space junk impact within this mountain range. Some communication from this case was also highlighted in John Greenewald Jr's *The Black Vault* within his FOIA Document Archives. Unfortunately, the requested information we received from the USFS was not quite as accurate as what we have asked for. This is not uncommon when working on investigations of this type.

After gathering as much information as possible online, I decided that it was now time to visit the area in person. Field Investigator Phil Reynolds and I conducted an on-site investigation of the area on August 25, 2013. We parked the car off Pleasant Valley Road and proceeded to hike up the mountainside for approximately 3.5 miles one way to an elevation of approximately 1,100 feet above sea level. We were rewarded with a beautiful scenic rocky overlook.

What would cause a piece of a large rock to break away - heat or an impact?

Norman Gagnon 8/25/2013

We took multiple photographs in the area of blackened trees and other charred remains. We found one large stone that had been split in two revealing its untainted inner core; unexposed to the elements, i.e. lichen growth. Was this caused by the intense heat of a forest fire or by an impact from a falling object? There were also two young trees outside the fire's path; although untouched by the flames, these trees were broken by some sort of direct force, both down trees were facing the same direction. Phil and I searched the mountaintop for any metallic debris but found nothing.

However, we didn't leave without a parting gift. Upon our return from the mountain top in the evening, we discovered that our legs were covered with hundreds of tiny Trombiculidae welts, also known as chigger bites that had been feeding on our skin.

Below is the MUFON field investigation final report based on this case. The folks that provided information for this report are posted below, initials only were used for most eyewitnesses involved. The MUFON field investigator who prepared the final report was Victor Rodriguez.

Warren County Report is based in the city of Front Royal and the newspaper covered the fire extensively in its 2012 mid-July edition.

Final Report by MUFON Field Investigator Victor Rodriguez – 2013

Synopsis:

A fire was reported within the George Washington & Jefferson National Forest on June 25, 2012, around 1 p.m. The fire was not extinguished until July 3, 2013. By that date, 1163 acres had been consumed. The event was covered by local TV Stations and the local newspapers. The most extensive coverage was in *The Warren County Report* in its mid-July 2012 edition, (Vol VII, issue 14).

281

Approximately one year after the event, MUFON Virginia State Director Susan L. Swiatek received an email from a MUFON member in Front Royal, Virginia, to make her aware of the reports that a UFO had been reported descending into the area and could have been the possible cause of the fire. Susan assigned three investigators to the case hoping that additional information could be shed on the event, (Norman Gagnon – STI, Phil Reynolds, and Victor Rodriguez.)

Background:

The George Washington National Forest includes 1.8 million acres in three states (Virginia, West Virginia, and Kentucky). Most of the forest land is in the state of Virginia. The community most directly affected by the fire was Front Royal, Virginia, about 70 miles west of Washington DC.

Description of the Event:

There was one main reporter covering the event for the local newspaper, Roger Bianchini. He interviewed the George Washington Information Offices, local fire officials, and eyewitnesses to the event. One of the eyewitnesses that came forward was MH, a local that resides on the west side of Front Royal about seven miles from the fire's point of origin. MH reported that about 11:50 p.m. he witnessed an object descend right into the area where the fire started. Also interviewed was CH, MH's cousin, who drove up to the fire with friends to get a better look at the site. He stated that at the top of the mountain, they encountered a moderate-sized flatbed truck hauling a tarp-covered object out of the area. He added that he was made aware of a message picked up by a scanner device inquiring about an ETA to Mt Weather, the FEMA facility in Clarke County.

Investigation:

In order to dismiss the obvious, under the Freedom of Information Act, inquiries were made to the Forest Service as to the causes of the fire and to NORAD (North American Aerospace Defense Command) to discount the possibility of space debris falling into the area.

The National Forest Service referred to the incident as the Point 2 Fire. Their conclusion was as follows: *"The cause of the fire was determined to be from lightning, due to the remoteness of the area and the lightning strike data that is collected by the Bureau of Land Management"*. A lightning strike map was provided. It showed the perimeter of the fire and the point of origin of the fire. There was indeed a lightning strike indicated on the site but <u>13 days earlier</u>. This is also reflected in the firefighter's log. *"Locals saw lightning – could have struck a few weeks back."*

Weather for the day in question was as follows: Partly Sunny with a high temperature of 80 and a low of 62 Fahrenheit. The same conditions were reported for the 24th to 27th of the month. There was no precipitation on any of the days. All the eyewitnesses interviewed agreed that the <u>weather was not a factor and lightning was definitely not a cause</u>.

NORAD was unresponsive to any of the inquiries about whether the fire was possibly caused by space debris falling into the area.

<u>Examination of the Site:</u>
Norman Gagnon and Phil Reynolds traveled to the site to see it firsthand. Due to the elapsed time, (over a year), a thorough search of the overlook area was conducted but no metallic debris was found.

<u>Field Investigator Victor Rodriguez – Interview of Eyewitnesses</u>
In the chance that Roger Bianchini, the reporter that broke the story, could shed some additional information on how to locate M and CH, Victor Rodriguez arranged for an interview with *The Warren County Reporter* in Front Royal. Mr. Roger Bianchini is a well-known personality in the Front Royal community. When asked how he arrived at the information that a UFO could be the cause of the fire, he indicated that MH had contacted him with the information. He was asked to recall the weather at the time of the fire and whether lightning was a possible cause. He remembers the day as being clear and sunny. When told that lightning was the cause according to the Forest Service he volunteered that based on the description of the event it was likely to be the crash of an

unmanned aircraft. I was able to contact the main witness MH by phone. I read the statement published by the newspaper. "At first it looked like a small crescent, like a crescent moon. Then as it was falling it became elongated until it came down on Massanutten Mountain. When it came down, there was an orange glow right from the area the fire was first reported in the next day."

When asked to recount what he remembered, he added: "I was exiting my parent's home around 11 p.m. on Sunday, June 24, 2012. Something caught my eye up in the sky. It had the shape of a waning moon but bright red in color. I soon realized it was up in the sky and descending fast. The object took 4 to 5 seconds to reach the ground. As the object descended it appeared to leave a trail. As it came down you could see the glow from behind the trees. There was no noise related to the event but I felt a rush of air that would be characteristic of a shock wave. Twelve hours later there was smoke emanating from the same area. My father was the first person to notify the fire department of the event."

When asked if CH had also witnessed the event, he added: "CH did not witness the event but he went up the mountain with me to see what was going on with the fire. There were quite a few people trying to do the same thing." MH was asked about the possibility that the fire could have been started by lightning. "The day of the fire was sunny and bright and there was no threat of precipitation. The previous evening was clear and you could see the stars.

There were no storms in the area and there was a light breeze."

He added that he had a friend who took a photo of the object as it came down. M was able to forward the photo taken by a friend of a girlfriend. The person that took the photo with her cell phone was away in school and could not be interviewed.

CH was interviewed in person. He was asked to recall the event. "We were up early. At sunrise, a plume of light smoke could be seen coming out of the forest. As time went by, it became a roaring fire. We decided to go up to the mountain to see what was going on. When we got up to Pleasant Valley Road, we saw a flatbed truck heading out of the area. In its bed, there was a large tarp covering something. The truck was accompanied by two SUVs. As we tried to get closer to the fire, we were directed to turn around. The person who asked us to turn around was not a policeman or fireman. The vehicles involved did not have markings identifying them with any agency."

He was asked about the scanner. "The scanner is owned by a friend. He let us know that he heard a request for an estimated time of arrival to Mount Weather. They assumed it was the vehicle they had seen leaving the scene of the fire."

It is hard to determine the reliability of the radio call. Mount Weather is listed as a FEMA facility. Little is known about the facility except that it is one of the locations where the federal government can relocate in case of a national emergency and no visitors or reporters are allowed in or around the facility. If something classified were to crash in the area, Mount Weather would be the logical ultimate destination.

Evaluation of Eyewitness

Both MH and CH are in their early twenties. M works for his father as an equipment operator in the Front Royal area. When approached on the phone, he expressed that he was surprised a government agency had not tried to contact him about the event.

CH is twenty years old and works for a construction company in northern Virginia. He is still puzzled by what he witnessed on top of Massanutten Mountain. SF was the source of the photograph, she is in her freshman year in college and a good friend of HE who knows MH well.

FI Victor Rodriguez: Conclusion

There was a large fire in the George Washington Forest that was reported on June 25, 2012, and was active until July 3, 2012. The official cause of the fire was lightning, see the USDA Forest Service Final Report dated July 7, 2012. Based on the interview of witnesses and weather records, and the lightning map provided by the agency, lightning was the most unlikely cause of the fire. Local newspaper coverage of the event made us aware of an eyewitness to an object descending into the forest where the fire originates the following morning. The following day there are reports of an object being transported under a tarp by a truck out of the area, a truck with a tarp-covered object is being escorted by two vehicles. The entire area is closed to the public. Whatever was being removed necessitated a security escort. A transmission was intercepted that someone or something is heading towards the Mt Weather facility. The source or content of transmission cannot be verified.

There was a single witness to the object descending into the mountain. A photo was provided but the source cannot be verified. However, a fire was detected in the location where the object impacted the ground early the following morning. There are no reports of downed aircraft or space debris. It is highly unlikely that such information would be made public under any circumstance. Based on the above we categorize this event as "Unknown".

End of report.

I discovered that through the years of investigating the countless of strange and unusual sightings that every so often make national news, there are many details that I ask myself that are not disclosed in these articles. Often, the best sources to obtain this information from the actual towns' small gazettes where these mysterious incidents have taken place.

You'll be surprised by the interesting tidbits you might also discover by simply emailing the local librarian or Sheriff's Department. As for the federal agency sources as to the Freedom of Information Act (FOIA) requests, whatever they decide to send you (or not) may reveal insight into what they are trying to sidestep or elude. For new field investigators, follow the '5Ws and 1H' guidelines, the who, what, when, where, and why, along with how. This will be a great start to develop your modus operandi of gathering crucial information for any investigations.

Chapter Eleven: Travel Log

"Travel is about the gorgeous feeling of teetering in the unknown."
– Anthony Bourdain

The following accounts are from my regional and global travels that highlight my interesting discoveries and capturing a few unexpected curiosities on film. In the course of my explorations, I believe it is also essential in taking a little time away from tracking shadows and to feed a different passion and that will be savoring indigenous foods, as you might have sighted in my earlier chapters.

Mysterious Canadian Power Outage – 1971

When I was 11 years old, I joined my mom on a summer vacation trip from Maryland to Canada, to visit relatives for a few weeks. She first dropped me off at my cousin's farmhouse in the rural area of Saint-Côme-Linière, which had a beautiful and wide expanse to run freely. Mom, on the other hand, stayed at our grand'mère house in the next town over as she also planned to visit other relatives in the area.

After my first exciting day of exploring the field of dreams, my cousin Rémy and I ran in to the supper table to have a meal of fried bologna with homegrown boiled potatoes, with a thick slice of bread on the side from the local bakery 'La Boulangerie Gailuron'. Our hearty meal was washed down with a tall glass of diluted unsweetened condensed milk.

Upon one evening, we were sitting in the living room with Uncle Roland in front of the black and white television set. We were about forty minutes into a movie and 'Thwack!"…we were in total darkness. The three of us were sitting in pitch black when the rotary phone unexpectedly began to ring. The interesting thing was that rather than the typical phone ring, it was a single continuous bell tone. What freaked me out the most is how much it reminded me of an emergency alarm. We sat in darkness for about a minute with this ringing constantly blaring before my uncle was able to find the phone cord and unplug it from the wall. Much to my relief, the electricity came on a short time later.

Rémy and I watched as my uncle got up from the sofa and walked to his bedroom. We heard some rustling and a door close. Soon, Uncle Roland returned from his bedroom holding a rifle! Without a word, he walked through the front screen door and down the porch steps. He paced a bit further into the dirt driveway. We uneasily followed him outside and watched him look at the darkened fields and up at the sky. With his best Chuck Connor's 'The Rifleman' expression, Uncle Roland turned around, gazed at both of us, and muttered in French, "Eh bien, nous avons dû manquer ces soucoupes volantes!", which roughly translated to, "Well, we must have just missed those darn flying saucers."

Not knowing what else to do, Rémy and I smiled nervously at each other and walked back into the house. It was unsettling how dark it was outside my uncle's farmhouse. It was too dark, especially after hearing him talk about a potential alien invasion.

After remembering this incident over thirty years later in 2002, I decided to search online for this 1970s power failure near my uncle's area. To my amazement, I found an internet Canadian article written by Claude MacDuff entitled *"Canadian Power Failures and UFO Sightings: An inquiry into the possible relationship between the presence of UFOs and electricity failures in Québec Province in July 1971."* Apparently, the power outages may have been caused by UFOs after all!

The article read that there were several French-Canadian newspapers in the Province de Québec reported inexplicable aerial sightings that correlated with power outages between July 18th and 24th, 1971. For example, a news story that appeared on July 23, 1971, edition of the newspaper *Le Devoir* detailed a sighting from near Rimouski, which is a city located in the Bas-Saint-Laurent region of Québec. According to the article, many witnesses saw round, unidentified flying objects that continuously flashed in alternating red, green, and blue lights. The more I researched, the more information I found that documented several power failures that coincided with UFO sightings in the region, including one that occurred over the electrical power station of the Hydro-Québec Company.

Back to my experience at the farm. I never heard my uncle Roland speak of flying saucers or space visitors before or after our unexpected power failure. Although that was the case, he did express a great interest in the historic Apollo 11 landing when we all sat in front of his old television set two years earlier. To this day, I am uncertain what motivated him to act as he did during this blackout, as he mysteriously uttered "flying saucer" while gazing upward at the night's sky. Perhaps this wasn't his first encounter, I mean his farmhouse is miles away from the main town, but I'll never know because we really did not strike up too many conversations.

My encounter with this odd electrical disturbance in Québec, Canada, was one of my first experiences with paranormal-related events that had been later documented by several Canadian articles and eyewitness reports. It opened my eyes to something that was much bigger than myself. It helped lead me into the investigative field and to take an interest in the paranormal. The light might have gone out for a few minutes at my uncle's farmhouse fifty years ago but my curiosity was lit up from inside that is still guiding me to the world of the unknown.

1995 Mexico Trip

In the summer of 1995, I joined my uncle René Gagnon for a week-long trip to Mexico for a little rest and relaxation. While the first couple of days were a bit nerve-racking, we did finally relaxed to enjoy the rest of our excursion. As Ralph Waldo Emerson once said, *"It's not the destination, it's the journey."*

First 48 hours

We flew from Washington, D.C. to Dallas-Fort Worth International Airport without incident. In Dallas, we transferred to a Mexican airline for a two-hour flight to Mexico City. As we prepared to land at the Mexico City International Airport tarmac, the plane suddenly banked sharply to the left about 60+ degrees. A couple of small carry-on bags tumbled from overhead compartments and a few passengers let out audible gasps and shrieks. As I collected my bearings, the plane leveled itself for another try at the airport's runway as I heard the engines rev up. I checked on my uncle sitting on my left, but he appeared to be focused on reading a newspaper article. He then folded the newspaper, leaned over to me, and calmly said, "Maybe a herd of goats had the right of way". As to Sir Roger Moore, I suppose that this was his way of jesting in the face of death.

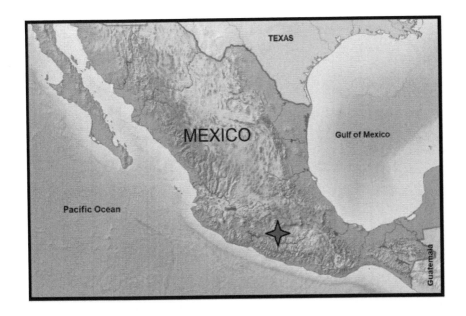

After we landed, Uncle René and I caught an outdated bus for our three-hour ride to Tejupilco de Hidalgo. I dozed off through the first hour of the mountainous jaunt, but when I woke up I found that the bus had stopped. I noticed that a few passengers had gotten off the bus and were standing to the side of the bus chattering.

I looked out my window and saw a colorfully dressed woman holding up a few tied plastic bags filled with effervescent yellow liquid, each with a straw pierced through the top. She was one of the few vendors that paced back and forth along the side of the bus; they were eager to sell refreshments to any passengers inside through their open windows. Not wanting to know what was in these lukewarm bags, I thought, "I'm good, gracias," and leaned back into my seat for the remainder of the excursion.

Next, I woke up by a nudge from my uncle's elbow, as we had arrived at a colorful adobe-style hotel on the outskirts of Tejupilco. After checking in, my uncle and I went to our rooms for the evening to recuperate from our long journey.

I was awakened early the next morning by the calls of tropical birds. I took a quick shower and left a fifty peso tip in the basket on my nightstand. Uncle René and I stepped out of our rooms and met for breakfast. As we were looking around for a place to eat, we walked across from the hotel where we found a street vendor who sold pajarete, a regional drink made from goat's milk, mango, instant coffee, and a variety of other ingredients whipped into a smoothie-like drink. Although most pajarete recipes may call for tequila, I did not detect any fermented agave in my delectable drink, but this thick morning beverage was enough to keep us going until lunch.

Afterward, we went to the nearby Plaza Hidalgo, where I took some 35mm photographs of the plaza. One remarkable photo, in particular, was of the sunrise peeking over the roof of the Templo de San Pedro Apostol, an early church built in the late 1500s. The photo result was phenomenal; the sun appeared as mystifying as the photos I have seen of the Virgin of Guadalupe or Marian Apparitions in the shape of a glowing figure!

296

Norman Gagnon © 1995

   With the aid of a cab driver, Uncle René and I explored the
subtropical valley in the western area of the State of Mexico
(the region where the indigenous Aztec peoples once thrived). This
was a forty-five-minute drive that led us into the municipality of
Santo Tomás de los Plátanos. As we drove along the road that
followed the edge of the river created by the dam at Presa Santa
Barbara, I was stunned to see what appeared to be a church steeple
exposed from the middle of this waterway! Here's a little
historical gem about this phantom cupola.

   The base of this valley once contained a village surrounded
by many orchards and coffee plantations. The tallest structure was
the church that so caught my attention.

The valley was intentionally flooded in 1956 by the Mexican government as part of a newly constructed dam project to hold water a few kilometers away. The old village was flooded in a matter of days which left only the tower topped with a cross that is still visible above the waterline. The larger expansion of water is located about 12 miles east of this submerged village that is now called Lake Avándaro next to the town of Valle de Bravo.

Norman Gagnon © 1995

A few hours before sunset, we drove back for about an hour to our final destination, the small villa of Luvianos. My uncle first made a quick stop at the edge of town and asked the cab driver to wait for a few minutes so he could show me a plot of land he purchased on top of a small mountain. He said that this was where he's going to build his homestead in a few months and to retire there.

The classic VW Beetle cab then took us back to the center of Luvianos and upon our arrival, we reserved two rooms at the Posada Familiar Buenavista hotel for the remainder of the week.

The view from outside my hotel's second-floor window, I could see below a bakery with a large window with an opened awning, as they were preparing traditional Mexican pan dulce or conchas, which is a sweet bread roll that comes in a variety of topped flavors. Shortly after sundown, we stepped out onto the street and we were taken in by the aromas of the sidewalk food vendors. The scents from a variety of sizzling antojitos being prepared all around us were amazing. Hunger was upon us! Within a few minutes, we heard what sounded like firecrackers...*pop, pop, pop*!

With excitement, I thought to myself, "They're having some sort of fiesta!" We looked around to see what was happening and realized that this was not the sound of celebration. The popping noises came from an old man with a rifle, in the center of the main square randomly firing shots over people's heads! My uncle and I ran to take cover behind a nearby Toyota truck. Before long, a camión full of Policía Mexicana arrived at the scene. They immediately jumped off the rear of the truck's flatbed and chased the old man away. When we determined that the main street was safe from stray bullets, we stood up and resumed our culinary stroll. Shortly after, we were enjoying the most delicious tostadas and authentic tacos that I have ever had in my life!

Exploring Nova Scotia -1996

In the summer of 1996, I had the yearning to visit Nova Scotia to do some exploration and to enjoy a couple nights out camping under the natural nightscape for some stargazing, unobscured by the haze of the city.

I packed my Chevy Beretta with a tent, a change of clothing, and a box of granola bars. After making some other last-minute preparations, threw on my safari vest and jumped onto northern Virginia's I-95, and drove up north about 850 miles non-stop to a rest stop in the state of Maine for a couple hours' shut-eye. When I woke up a few hours later from my reclined seat, I discovered that my front left tire was flat. I figured that I must have picked up a souvenir of a sharp metal fragment of road debris in Secaucus, New Jersey. As I recall I had to swerve to avoid an abandoned car wreck that slightly obstructed the left lane of the highway.

After a phone call to a local garage to have my flat tire fixed and with a hardy vending machine breakfast, I soon crossed the border of Canada. I resumed my journey northeast through the province of New Brunswick. A few hours later, I arrived at the western peninsula seaboard of Nova Scotia, one of Canada's eastern provinces.

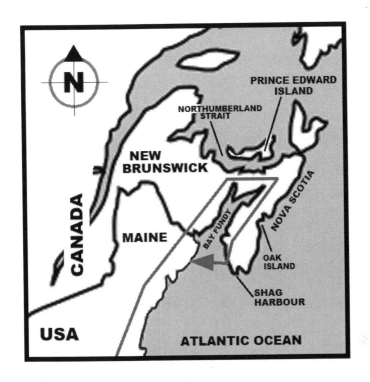

Continuing easterly on NS-104 for 40 miles or so then made a sharp right turn onto Hwy 215 that hugged the scenic shoreline of western Nova Scotia. I drove further past my fourth *"We Have Fresh Blueberries"* signs and after a few more hours' drive, I could see the sun started to set behind the New Brunswick sea cliffs on the other side of the Bay of Fundy, which is the body of water that separates the province of New Brunswick from Nova Scotia.

I did not really plan where I was going to spend the night, but I soon came upon a road sign for a small campground, so I gave this place a try. After registering, I found a secluded spot to set up my small dome tent, right next to wild blueberry bushes. After sundown, I laid on top of a picnic table and stared at the sky to catch glimpses of our universe above. After a while, I went to my tent to settle in for the night. The cool breeze blowing through the screen was invigorating and delightedly pure.

Norman Gagnon © 1996

Early the next morning, I walked over to the registration cabin to check out. After paying, I walked over a few feet to the café for breakfast. Oddly enough, I had a craving for blueberry pancakes. My platter soon came with two thick strips of crispy bacon with real maple syrup on the side, and a remarkable cup of black coffee. After my delicious déjeuner, I packed my tent and resumed motoring southwestward on Route 209 overlooking the bay on my right. Before long, I arrived near Advocate Harbor where I planned to visit the Cape D'Or Lighthouse and maybe do a little fossil hunting upon the basalt cliffs. I found a spot to park my car and was about to walk down the trail to the lighthouse below.

When I opened the car door, I heard a continuous rumbling coming from a hill behind me. Curiosity taking the best of me, I immediately decided to take a peek at what was causing this uproar. Without thinking twice, I climbed up the side of a small but steep hill toward the spruce trees that lined the top. When I reached the crest of the hill, I got hit with a powerful air current from the coastal wind that sounded like a freight train!

I resumed towards the drop-off until I came upon the boundary of the cliff that must have had a drop of over 600 feet to the rocky shore below. I cautiously stepped away from the ledge enough so that I could safely enjoy the truly breathtaking view I had just found.

In silence, I imagined how this landscape might feel similar to the wild highlands of Scotland that is about 2,700 miles westward voyage from here. I thought of the first seaward explorers who settled in this area over 360 years ago and chose to name their new discovery Nova Scotia or 'New Scotland'. If this new land reminded them of home, I definitely had to plan a trip to Scotland one day.

Norman Gagnon © 1996

After taking in the view for several minutes, I climbed back down to the parking lot and walked the quarter-mile path to the Cape D'Or Lighthouse below. I took a few panoramic photos of the beautiful shore and rock formations that surrounded the lighthouse. The Cape D'Or Lighthouse began as a steam-powered foghorn station in 1874. A wooden tower was constructed on the site in 1922 and in 1965 a red lantern room on a white fortified concrete beacon was added. As I stood beside the lighthouse, a two-hundred-year-old local legend about a haunted ship came to mind.

Ghost Ship of Northumberland Strait

An interesting bit of the local history of the Maritime Provinces was that of the Ghost Ship of Northumberland Strait. This strait is the navigable waterway between the northern tip of Nova Scotia and Prince Edward Island.

For over two hundred years, the ghost ship has been described as a three-masted vessel said to be engulfed in flames seen near the rocky shores of the strait. Although one of the first documented accounts of the ship was recorded in the 17th century, there have been sightings from both sides of the strait as recently as a few years ago.

The first account of the ghost ship took place in the late 1800s. One foggy night, townspeople from nearby Charlottetown, a city located at the harbor in Prince Edward Island, were petrified to see the distant silhouette of a sailing vessel consumed in the fire! Several sailors jumped into a wooden rowboat to rush toward the burning schooner to rescue the crew. However, as they approached the location of the ship it disappeared in a thick fog. The story was covered in the longstanding Prince Edward Island *'The Charlottetown'* newspaper. The article is quoted as saying that 'people and dogs' were seen running on the deck of this ship before it disappeared into the mist.

Since that first reported sighting of the burning ship, there have been at least a dozen reputable eyewitness accounts of the Ghost Ship of Northumberland Strait. Here are two sightings that have taken place in more recent times.

Based on internet sources, the articles about the sighting were written by Kevin Mann Jr., a teacher at the area high school. On the evening of 10, 1980, Kevin looked across the bay of the Northumberland Strait with binoculars when a bright light on the water caught his attention. When he refocused his binoculars to get a clearer image, he saw a three-masted ship that appeared to be engulfed in orange flames. Mann did not believe in ghosts but did feel that what he saw was an unexplained 'light manifestation' of some sort.

Another mysterious sighting of the Ghost Ship of Northumberland Straight took place in February 2008. On this occasion, 17-year-old Mathieu Giguere was interviewed by *The Truro Daily News* about his own account with the legendary phantom ship. Mathieu said that he saw the burning vessel from the shore of Tatamagouche Bay which is part of the Northumberland Strait. Mathieu described the flames as 'bright white and gold' but became perplexed by what he saw because he realized that the bay was frozen solid and no ship could have been on the water at the time.

Garrison Cemetery – Annapolis Royal, Nova Scotia
Toward the end of my five-day excursion, I made a stopover to Fort Anne National Historic Site in Annapolis Royal to visit Garrison Cemetery which is located about twenty yards from Fort Anne's Fortress.

The Garrison Cemetery graveyard has one of the oldest English standing tombstones, which dates back to 1720. Most of the other stone markers have been weathered to the point where the names and dates are illegible. Among the tombstones were several wooden markers whose inscriptions have long since decayed. Archeologists have confirmed that an unmarked site near the cemetery is the final resting place for Acadian settlers from the mid-1600s.

The Acadians are the descendants of the native people and the French who settled in Acadia during the 17th and 18th centuries. Acadia was the name given to the area of the French colonial empire of New France in this region, which includes New Brunswick, Nova Scotia, Prince Edward Island, and the now state of Maine, which is where I was born in.

Fort Anne in the background. Norman Gagnon © 1996

As for Fort Anne, this territory was originally claimed by the Scots around 1629 but was overtaken by the French before it finally fell to British rule in 1710. This ground was the most fought-over piece of land in Canadian history since European colonization.

<u>Ghosts</u>

I am quite sure that this whole area oozes with ghostly stories mixed with historical events that have been told and retold. For example, Fort Anne also has offered Candlelight Graveyard Tours hosted by guides and interpreters to share the area's legends for all members of the family young and old, for over 30 years.

After leaving the cemetery, I returned to Route 101 and drove southwest toward my final Nova Scotian destination, the port town of Yarmouth. I stayed at a hotel for my final overnight rest and to enjoy a well-needed shower. For dinner, I had a large bowl of hodge-podge stew made with fresh vegetables with chunks of flaky white fish, with a small baguette on the side to soak up the amazing broth!

<u>Voyage back home</u>

I woke up early the next morning and drove into the Yarmouth Terminal where I had scheduled a ferryboat passage a few weeks prior. By 9:40 a.m., the ferryboat departed for the 98-nautical miles cruise across the Gulf of Maine and to the United

States. About fifteen minutes after departure, the sky suddenly became inexplicably dark as the boat was engulfed with an unexpected fog mixed with a light drizzle. This was definitely strange considering the sun was just shining just a few minutes before. It felt like I was in the beginning of a Steven Spielberg scenario.

On the ferryboat navigating through the thick fog. Norman Gagnon © 1996

As I walked along the port side of the deck and it dawned on me that just 35 miles to my left is the small fishing village of Shag Harbour. This small town had one of the most remarkable UFO or to be exact, a USO (Unidentified Submerged Object) incident on record. On October 4, 1967, several witnesses saw a bright yellow object impact the water near the southern shore of Nova Scotia. The light from the object was so bright that many locals thought it was an airplane crash.

Upon hearing of the report of a potential plane crash the Royal Canadian Mounted Police and Canadian military became involved in a joint search and rescue effort; though, no floating crash debris was found. However, they did find a mysterious yellow foam that floated on top of the water. Many who took part in the recovery reported seeing glowing lights underwater that appeared to be moving away from Shag Harbour and to the open sea toward the United States shore. They also noticed that the lights left a trail of the same yellow glowing foam.

After taking a few photos, I thought to myself, "Great, I'm on a boat surrounded by a mysterious fog and we appear to be heading on the same pathway as to this infamous incident involving an unexplained underwater vessel that vanished right under me".

After a moment, I knew what needed to be done. I went inside and took advantage of the onboard amenities, and ordered myself a cold Molson Ale. This ale is one of Canada's most popular beers from one of North America's oldest breweries founded in 1786 in Montréal City, in the province of Québec.

After nearly four hours, the ferry arrived at the shore of Bar Harbor, Maine. The sun then appeared from above as I got onto I-95 south to resume my travels back home to Northern Virginia.

Abandoned Coast Guard Lifesaving Station

Dare County, North Carolina

In the summer of 2004, I was driving south exploring the North Carolinas Outer Bank's NC 12 Scenic Byway that overlooks the shores of the Atlantic Ocean. The Outer Banks (OBX), also known as "The Graveyard of the Atlantic", is a string of barrier islands off the coast of the mainland that has had more than 2,000 shipwrecks due to some of the most treacherous waters in the world to navigate through and with the ever-shifting sands of the inlets.

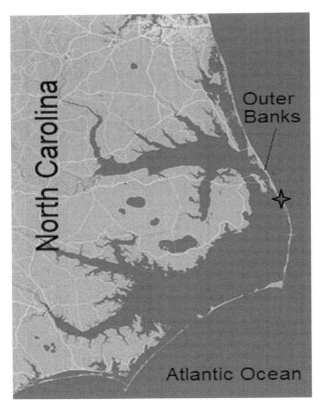

About a mile after crossing the Herbert C. Bonner Bridge, I noticed to my left the top of what appeared to be an old decrepit tower almost hidden behind a 25-foot sand dune. I thought to myself, "This place needs a quick reconnaissance!" I carefully made a left turn onto a barely noticeable sandy pathway, and I parked about 40 yards away from this abandoned wooden structure. After I got out of the car, I found a battered sign that read The Oregon Inlet Lifesaving Station.

Looking like a scene from a post-apocalyptic movie. Norman Gagnon © 2004

History of the Oregon Inlet Life Saving Station

The Oregon Inlet Life Saving Station was built in 1898 and was home to brave surf crews who rescued mariners who were shipwrecked or stranded in the dangerous waters beyond the breakers. From the time it opened until it closed more than ninety years later, the United States Coast Guard had remodeled the station at least twice. It was permanently closed and vacated in

312

1988 due to funding cutbacks and because it was too difficult and costly to maintain among the constant and shifting sand dunes that were adjacent to the shore. The historic station fell into disrepair and has slowly started to disappear into the sands of time.

Norman Gagnon © 2004

With my camera, I started walking towards the Quonochontaug-style building and came upon the top of a chain-link fence as its corner post cap was barely exposed above the sand. Some buried barbed wire also protruded out of the mound and several pieces of wooden debris were scattered near the front porch of the timeworn building. The station's windows and entrances were well boarded-up which prevented curiosity seekers from entering the building. As I walked over the west end of the station, I came upon a number of pointed, round-roofed structures that looked like grain silos. Later, I determined that they were cisterns half-buried in a dune among the scattered growth of the marram grass.

313

Norman Gagnon © 2004

I continued to walk around the perimeter of the station and after I passed the cisterns, I discovered an opening to what appeared to be a storage shed. To no surprise, it was filled with windblown sand that had forced its way inside. There were a few footprints left behind by other inquisitive sightseers who walked into the darkened storeroom that still contained the rusty remains of items used in days gone by.

Strange Markings on a Stone

On May 12, 2007, I was on an expedition with a few members of the Pennsylvania Bigfoot Society exploring the landscape at Loyalsock State Park in Sullivan County, Pennsylvania. On this particular outing, my colleagues and I were looking for the spoor (the tracks or scent) of an elusive Sasquatch that had recently been sighted in the area.

At Loyalsock State Park, Pennsylvania. Norman Gagnon © 2007

We drove up an old loggers' road about 19,000 feet to a scenic mountainous overlook and parked our vehicles. After investigating one area for a few minutes, I came upon the remains of shredded fur from what was once a rabbit left behind by some predatory creature that had been seemingly famished.

After about two hours or so, the team paced to an open area from the woods when I came upon a protruding stone that appeared to have been placed there intentionally.

I began to examine this grey trapezoid-shaped rock and the next thing I know, my archaeologist instinct kicked in. I estimated that it was approximately 22 inches tall, 30 inches long, and about 12 inches wide. Upon closer observation, there were two unusual grooves or petroglyphs chiseled into its angle side and top surface, resembling the key character '[' square brackets. Each symbol appeared to be about 1/8-inch-deep and about 3.5 inches long. The back of the stone had what appeared to be a 2-inch Egyptian hieroglyph symbol of the '*Reed leaf*' that seemed to have been etched into the back surface. Photographs and measurements were taken prior to our departure and a few of my teammates were wondering why I was intensely examining this rock. Although we did not find any signs of the Bigfoot creature, this strange stone did certainly pique my interest.

A hieroglyph-looking symbol of the reed leaf as noted with the graphic.
Norman Gagnon © 2007

After returning home from my expedition, I emailed a few specialists in Pennsylvania with backgrounds in ancient architecture and geology. However, they all were as perplexed as I was about the markings on the stone. Some said that these may have been quarry marks but I felt that was unlikely since the stone was at an elevation of 1,900 feet above sea level and with no signs of an open-pit mine in the whole area.

Although I hit a dead end with these experts, I was not about to give up on this mystery. I contacted a historian, independent researcher Terry J. Deveau that was a featured guest on the History Channel's '*The Curse of Oak Island.*' His conjecture was that it may have been a boundary marker of some kind. After he shared his observation, I agreed that it did appear to be the shape of a surveyor's stone of some sort. However, in my view, it seemed much, much older than the typical smooth carved stone markers. Customarily, surveyor stones have numbers or town initials carved into them…but these carvings appear to be age-old symbols. The hieroglyph-looking mark in the back could possibly be a directional arrow symbol. The thought that this old stone being a state boundary marker still does not fully make sense to me considering it was on top of an undeveloped mountain that was about thirty miles south of the New York state line.

Logan-Wallace Manor Paranormal Gathering

In the spring of 2016, I received an email from the Virginia MUFON Assistant Director Ben Moss about a potential investigation of the paranormal kind along with enjoying a little rest and relaxation in the neighboring state of Pennsylvania. Ben further explained that this meet and greet will not only encompass a team of UFO investigators but also ghost hunters!

Ken Ballos, a retired Deputy Sheriff from Richmond, Virginia, reached out to Ben with a tantalizing proposal of gathering the best of the best field researchers within the Washington D.C. area and to investigate a 100-year-old haunted manor. The proprietor of this grand English Tudor mansion was our very own Virginia MUFON Field Investigator Tony Angiola who agreed to this madness. The team members that were part of this investigative venture were as follows:

Ben Moss and Tony Angiola: Top UFO Field Investigators and both were also hosts of the 2015 History Channel documentary TV series, *Hangar 1: The UFO Files.*

<u>Ken Ballos</u>: Ex enforcement officer that established his own team of Ghost Hunters in the capital city of Richmond, Virginia, called Richmond Investigators of the Paranormal (RIP). He was also the host of *RIP Paranormal Talk Radio Show*. Two young ladies of the RIP team also joined Ken on this weekend's investigation.

<u>Wilbur Allen</u>: A Scientist/Analyst/Field Researcher and Segment Producer for The History Channel, who brought with him some serious field equipment.

<u>Norman Gagnon</u>: Former licensed Private Investigator and current Paranormal Investigator, guest MUFON STAR Team Field Investigator in an episode of the 2008 Discovery Channel documentary series, *'UFOs Over Earth – Fayetteville Incident'* episode.

Early Friday morning of May 27, 2016, we packed our vehicles for our 300-mile northwest drive to the Historic District of Warren, Pennsylvania. About 5.5 hours later, we pulled in the rear gated circular driveway of this grand house, as my first thought was, "This looks like the Wayne Manor from the 1960's TV series *'Batman'* starring Adam West!"

Tony Angiola's Manor House.   Norman Gagnon © 2016

History: City of Warren

This notable town is located along the Allegheny River, a locality that was initially inhabited by Native Americans of the Seneca Nation. In the late 1790s, lumbering quickly became the town's main industry until the discovery of oil in a nearby town in 1859, which marked Warren's passage from a small rural town to an advanced industrial community.

Logan-Wallace Manor

Prior to the construction of this manor, there was a wood-framed warehouse on this site used as a temporary assembly for the Jordan Tabernacle Church in the mid-19-hundreds. Between 1918 and 1920, the three-story dwelling was built that comprised 6,700 square feet of living space, not included the large, finished basement. Scottish masons had to be imported to Pennsylvania to fabricate these intricate 13-inch-thick walls. This stately manor was built for oil baron Harry A. Logan. Four additional owners occupied this estate until the keys were dropped in Tony's opened hand in 2001 as he became the current proprietor. Although he now owns the manor, he has to share it with whatever is secretly lurking in the shadows of this historical architecture.

As Tony unlocked the rear entrance doors, Ben and I walked through grinning in awe while we dropped our gear in the foyer as the anticipated tour of this chateau soon followed. Beautiful wood paneling with molded ceilings was everywhere. The leaded casement windows lit the way to the formal living room that displayed a massive marble fireplace and yes, there were secret compartments hidden in the paneling! No bust of Shakespeare was discovered anywhere though. I later chose one of the four bedrooms on the second-floor for my bedchamber as I unrolled my air mattress and unpacked my gear.

A week prior to our casual weekend investigation, I built myself a custom "gear-gauntlet" consisting of affixed K2 Electromagnetic EMF Field Meter, Digital Thermometer (ambient temperature reader), and a Pelican ProGear LED flashlight that were affixed to it.

The rationale behind this augmented ghost-hunting apparatus is simply to keep my hands free so I can freely utilize my digital camera, or maybe handle a large slice of NYC pizza while I saunter about in the dark.

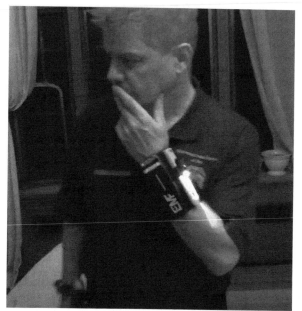

Testing my prototype Gear-Gauntlet © 2016

Manor Ghostly Accounts:

Tony shared a disturbing incident involving his stepson, who had long hair at the time. In 2006, late one night as he was walking from the library to the kitchen to get a snack. While he passed through the darkened corridor that led to the main kitchen, something grabbed his ponytail and tugged it. Furious by this prank, he ran upstairs to complain and found Tony and his mom quietly watching television.

Both were very surprised by this and they replied that they were in the master bedroom for a few hours relaxing. His stepson's expression changed from anger to sheer terror!

With a little detective work, I found that Mr. John C. Wallace Sr. has a son named Jack Wallace. I sent him an email in the summer of 2021 to get his take on what went on behind these turn-of-the-century walls since the Wallaces moved out in 1972.

Jack wrote back, "We kids always thought the house was haunted…but not in a bad way. But we heard a lot of curious noises and some belongings would get mysteriously moved about. The story was that Harry Logan Sr. had built the house for a first love (or wife) who died before it was finished, but that she took up residence in it anyway. My sisters and I always had the sense that the presence was female, benign, and very turn-of-the-century lady-like.

The grand living room. © 2016

Ken and his RIP team got turned around a little during their late Friday night arrival in Warren and had to rest for the night. Luckily, they did show up at the manor early Saturday morning, with Wilbur Allen soon to follow as he also parked next to the carriage house. After we enjoyed a large breakfast at a local restaurant, we returned to prep our equipment for the night's ghost (and UFO) hunt.

Our equipment included three different types of EMF (electro-magnetic field) detectors, several digital cameras, digital thermometers, motion sensor devices, two laser grid pens, and a spirit-box (an audio device that rapidly scans through multiple radio stations for ghosts to use to "communicate" with the user by choosing words or phrases from any of the channels, in real-time.) There were two-night vision camcorders mounted on tripods that were set up in both the living room pointing towards the kitchen entryway and at the top of the second-floor main stairwell facing the master bedroom door that also had a motion sensor light placed on the floor to detect movement from any spectral anomalies.

9:45 p.m.: Lights out – Hunt's on

I chose to start in the basement as the temperature was much cooler as expected, while I checked my digital thermometer. As I passed the boiler room and further down the shadowy hall, I saw a large black metal door to my left with yellow letters painted on its surface: '*Cary Safe Co., Buffalo, NY*'. This was the manor's walk-in vault. There were also other rooms on each side of me that had different uses, such as for storing dried goods, the laundry room, and a sunken exercise/rec room at the other end of the basement. After a while, I did hear undefined noises within this darkened cellar.

Not too long after, I heard screams from the first floor above that were followed by a quick radio check. It appeared that a bat was frantically flying around the living room trying to find a way out, while the two RIP young ladies were trying to dodge this fluttering beast. Fortunately, the bat was gently captured with a soft towel and safely released outside.

Every hour or so, we would switch floors and take turns to investigate other levels, as each floor seemed to have its own eerie impressions.

Ben Moss' Preliminary Ghost Hunt

Ben, at 6'-2" and at 220-pounds, wasn't too shy about trying this new investigative pursuit. He grabbed a digital recorder and climbed the narrow back staircase to the third floor to try this out, solo.

The third floor was originally used as servant quarters with three bedrooms, one bath, a walk-in cedar closet, a sewing room with a wall of built-in cabinets, and several storage areas. With his flashlight turned off and within a minute of being cloaked in total darkness, he soon felt a menacing presence shortly after his first EVP question and left my digital recorder running.

When we talked to Ben later, he told us of his amazing experience. "I began by speaking out loud that I was not scared, and I was not harmful in any way. I would say 'come talk to me' or 'tap me on the shoulder' if you're here. I could barely see more than a foot in front of me. Suddenly, I had a distinct feeling that I was being watched, yet I was all alone at the back end of the hall, next to an open door of the master bedroom. The hair on the back of my next was rising, and I started to get a little nervous.

I kept turning to look behind me, where there was only the back wall of the house and the open bedroom doorway. In an instant, I felt that someone or something was right over my left shoulder. I stayed another 10 minutes and then went downstairs to talk to the group. We played the EVP recording back, and at about the moment when I had felt a presence behind me, someone had whispered, apparently right up close to the recorder, 'Ben'. It was clear that my name was called, and it was like a whisper in my ear, but I only heard it when we played the recording back."

I'd like to add that Harry A. Logan was 6'- 6" tall, which is just about the same height as Ben. Perhaps when Ben was wandering about the top floor in the dark, his tall silhouette may have appeared familiar to the spirit that occupied the third floor.

Ben's second incident was when we were on the main floor, as RIP was conducting an EVP with their Spirit-Box. Ben, "I was told that there were not a lot of words programmed into the device, and certainly not my name. But, as we were trying to get it to speak to us, it said 'Ben friend'. Ken, one of our fellow investigators from Richmond, said the name Ben was not in the device. But I felt good that whatever was there in our presence considered me friendly, as it was my nature."

Ben's third incident was just as startling. Ben, "This happened at around 3 AM as we were all sitting outside winding down from the long day and night. Norm was in front of me as was Tony, sitting in beach chairs in the early morning hours. I was behind them next to the back entrance of the house, where there was a large brick façade. All of us were outside at the time. Suddenly, clear as a bell, a voice, in my estimation, about 10 feet in the air behind me, said 'Ben' very loud. Norm said, "Did you just say that?" I was about to ask them the same thing. But the direction of where the voice came from was up and to my left, where there are no windows, nothing but a wall. At that point I guess these ghosts were still interested in me in particular, perhaps because I was always trying to be open and friendly, joking around a lot." The manor's secluded boarder by the name of Jack Daniels may have quietly introduced himself during the wee morning hours, to contribute in providing a little warmth to a few investigators sitting outside in the cool summer breeze.

Wilbur on the other hand had set up both of his ISO 204800 and ISO 409600 infrared/full-color night vision cameras outside, one of which was aiming straight up at the night sky. These camera sensors could pick up visible, infrared, and ultraviolet light, and pretty much capturing the entire spectrum, as the footage results looked very sharp, clean, and focused. These types of cameras are also utilized in law enforcement agencies for collecting data and evidence at crime scenes.

328

In fact, there was a video footage that clearly captured two unidentified aerial objects flying high above, one glowing object slightly ahead of the other, soaring swiftly across the stratosphere. No contrails seen or distance rumbling of jet engines heard on this footage.

Later, our ghostly results have revealed that a few of us heard the sound of a creaking basement door being slightly ajar for a few seconds but as to an audible alarm, the rusty hinges put a stop at whatever was trying to sneak in undetected. Ben seems to have attracted a spirit that kept calling for him. RIP's video footage captured the motion sensor light turn on, at the top of the 2nd-floor main stairwell near the entrance of the master bedroom. Perhaps it was activated by a specter that may have hovered through.

During the course of the investigation, while the manor's lights were still out, Tony saw one of the living room sconces simply lit up.

May 29th, Sunday morning's ride back

Two hours into our drive back to Virginia, our host Tony decided to make a quick stop at one of his favorite bar-b-q joints, right off highway I-80 called Gio's BBQ, in Woodland, PA, for some flavorful takeout. We chose to order the least messy platter on the menu as we needed to quickly get back on the interstate without the risk of smearing their award-winning BBQ sauce or related juices all over the car's interior. So, we all ordered the smoked hot sausage with sautéed onions and green peppers, wrapped in a protective hoagie bun, and with a side of coleslaw.

This was a perfect recipe to conclude our sensational weekend of amigos, antiquity, and apparitions!

***

"Previous experience had taught me that any expedition marches on its stomach." — Tahir Shah

"Exploration is curiosity put into action."
- Don Walsh.

Fort Pickens, Santa Rosa Island, Pensacola, Florida. Norman Gagnon © 2021

FIN

Made in the USA
Middletown, DE
24 October 2022

13344995R00186